Ninja Air Fryer
Cookbook for Beginners UK

Simple & Delicious Recipes with Photos | The Ultimate Guide & Tips and Tricks of Ninja Air Fryer | UK Measurements | FULL-COLOR

Glenda Hand

© Copyright 2024-All Rights Reserved.

This document is geared towards providing exact and reliable information concerning the topic and issue covered. The publication is sold with the idea that the publisher is not required to render accounting, officially permitted, or otherwise, qualified services. If advice is necessary, legal or professional, a practiced individual in the profession should be ordered.

In no way is it legal to reproduce, duplicate, or transmit any part of this document in either electronic means or in printed format. Recording of this publication is strictly prohibited, and any storage of this document is not allowed unless with written permission from the publisher. All rights reserved.

The information provided herein is stated to be truthful and consistent, in that any liability, in terms of inattention or otherwise, by any usage or abuse of any policies, processes, or Instructions: contained within is the solitary and utter responsibility of the recipient reader. Under no circumstances will any legal responsibility or blame be held against the publisher for any reparation, damages, or monetary loss due to the information herein, either directly or indirectly.

Respective authors own all copyrights not held by the publisher.

The information herein is offered for informational purposes solely and is universal as such. The presentation of the information is without a contract or any type of guarantee assurance.

The trademarks that are used are without any consent, and the publication of the trademark is without permission or backing by the trademark owner. All trademarks and brands within this book are for clarifying purposes only, are owned by the owners themselves, and are not affiliated with this document.

Contents

1 Introduction 1

2 Fundamentals of Ninja Air Fryer Max XL 2

3 4-Week Meal Plan 13

4 Chapter 1 Breakfast................. 15

15 Cheesy Bacon Egg Muffins
15 Bacon and Eggs Breakfast
16 Cheese and Sausage Quiche
16 Spinach and Cheese Quiche
17 Flavourful Cheese Onion Risotto
17 Baked Pecan French Toast
18 Cheese Tomato Frittata
18 Sweet Cranberry Muffins
19 Apple Pancakes
19 Scrambled Eggs with Mushrooms
20 Fluffy Corn Bread
20 Homemade Pork Patties
21 Air Fried Scotch Eggs
21 Cheesy Egg Stuffed Peppers
22 Nut and Berry Granola
22 Glazed Ham Steak

5 Chapter 2 Vegetables and Sides ... 23

23 Air Fried Vegetable Skewers
23 Tasty Cheese Spinach Frittata
24 Crispy Turnip Fries
24 Tomato Avocado Boats
25 Cauliflower Pizza Crust
25 Cheese Soufflés with Mushrooms
26 Courgette Fritters
26 Homemade Roasted Brussels Sprouts with Bacon
27 Prosciutto-Wrapped Asparagus
27 Simple Courgette Ribbons
28 Garlic Broccoli with Sriracha
28 Healthy Tamari Green Beans
29 Roasted Brussels Sprouts
29 Garlic Roasted Cherry Tomatoes

6 Chapter 3 Snacks and Starters ... 30

30 Bacon-Wrapped Sausage
30 Fluffy Cloud Eggs
31 Broccoli Cheddar Casserole
31 Crispy Flax Cheddar Cheese Chips
32 Crispy Mozzarella Cheese Sticks
32 Garlicky Radish Chips
33 Buffalo Cauliflower Florets
33 Roasted Taco Cauliflower
34 Cheesy Cauliflower Bites
34 Rosemary Potato Chips with Sour Cream
35 Balsamic Roasted Brussels Sprouts
35 Cheese Drop Biscuits
36 Crunchy Spanish Peanuts
36 Pigs in a Blanket
37 Shakshuka Harissa
37 Tasty Masala Omelet

(7) Chapter 4 Poultry 38

38 Cajun Chicken Breasts
38 Marinated Chicken Drumsticks
39 Spicy Chicken Wings
39 Cheesy Chicken and Courgette Casserole
40 Flavourful Buffalo Chicken Wings
40 Easy Marinated Chicken Wings
41 Almond-Crusted Chicken Nuggets
41 Delicious Chicken Breasts
42 Buttermilk Fried Chicken Breasts
42 Crispy Chicken Nuggets
43 Buttermilk Fried Chicken Wings
43 Air Fryer Crispy Whole Chicken Wings
44 Crispy Popcorn Chicken
44 Lemon Roasted Whole Chicken
45 Turkey Breasts with Shallot

(8) Chapter 5 Seafood 46

46 Tasty Garlic Prawns
46 Savoury Tuna Kabobs
47 Crispy Fried Prawns
47 Lemon Salmon Skewers
48 Salmon with Coconut Avocado Sauce
48 Garlic Prawns with Pasta Alfredo
49 Roasted Lemon Prawns
49 Crispy Fish with Potato Wedges
50 Easy Roasted Sesame Prawns
50 Rosemary Prawns with Cherry Tomatoes
51 Tender Garlic Cod Fish
51 Pesto Fish Finger Burgers
52 Lemony Breaded Fish Fillets
52 Garlic Butter Lobster Tails
53 Blackberry Glazed Salmon
53 Spiced Catfish Fillets

(9) Chapter 6 Meat 54

54 Beef and Sausage Meatballs
54 Classic Meatloaf
55 Kofta Kebabs
55 Low-Carb Lasagna
56 Ham Mac 'N' Cheese
56 Air Fried Short Ribs
57 Homemade Cheeseburgers
57 Authentic Carne Asada
58 Simple Pork Bulgogi
58 Crispy Parmesan Pork Chops
59 Lamb Patties with Feta
59 Walnut-Crusted Pork Tenderloin
60 Perfect Beef Roast
60 Juicy Garlic Butter Steak
61 Air Fryer Marinated Steak

(10) Chapter 7 Desserts 62

62 Yummy Black 'n' White Brownies
62 Orange Polenta Cake
63 Sweet Banana Cake
63 Chocolate Chip Cookies
64 Chocolate Chip Macadamia Nut Cookies
64 Coconut Cream Cheese Muffins
65 Chocolate Soufflé
65 Mini Chocolate Cake
66 Vanilla Butter Cake
66 Easy Peanut Butter Cookies

(11) Conclusion 67

(12) Appendix Recipes Index 68

Introduction

Welcome to the Ninja Air Fryer Max XL Cookbook, your essential companion for unleashing the full potential of one of the most versatile kitchen appliances available today. Designed for the modern home cook, this cookbook is crafted to inspire you to create delicious, healthier meals with ease and confidence. The Ninja Air Fryer Max XL not only cooks your favourite dishes with a fraction of the oil traditionally used, but it also delivers remarkable taste and texture that will impress family and friends alike.

Within these pages, you will discover a diverse collection of recipes that cater to every palate, from crispy chips and golden roast potatoes to succulent meats and vibrant vegetable dishes. Each recipe has been carefully developed to take advantage of the air fryer's unique features, ensuring that you achieve perfect results every time. Whether you're a seasoned chef or new to the kitchen, our straightforward instructions and handy tips will guide you step by step. In addition to tantalising recipes, this cookbook contains how to use this appliance, making sure that your culinary skills are elevated.

Join us on this culinary adventure and discover the joys of cooking with the Ninja Air Fryer Max XL. With its ability to create quick, healthy, and delicious meals, this innovative appliance will soon become your go-to kitchen helper. Let's embark on a journey to transform your cooking experience, one crispy bite at a time!

Fundamentals of Ninja Air Fryer Max XL

Now is the perfect moment to delve into the essentials of the Ninja Air Fryer Max XL, where the harmonious blend of sizzle and simplicity meets a contemporary nod to tradition. This remarkable appliance is not just a kitchen tool; it functions as a maestro, orchestrating culinary masterpieces that elevate every meal. But what sets this culinary conductor apart? Are there hidden features waiting to be discovered? And how can you unlock all its potential?

Prepare yourself for an exciting exploration! This section will provide you with comprehensive insights into the Ninja Air Fryer Max XL. Grasping the fundamentals of this innovative appliance is crucial for unleashing its ability to produce outstanding textures, flavours, and delectable dishes. By understanding its core functionalities—such as its various cooking modes, temperature settings, and time controls—you will gain the confidence to experiment and create dishes that not only satisfy but also impress.

Join us on this enlightening journey as we uncover the secrets of the Ninja Air Fryer Max XL, transforming your cooking experience and making every meal a celebration of taste and creativity.

What is Ninja Air Fryer Max XL?

The Ninja Air Fryer Max XL is an innovative kitchen appliance designed to transform the way you cook, offering a versatile and health-conscious alternative to traditional frying methods. As a standout member of the Ninja family, known for its commitment to quality and functionality, this air fryer boasts a range of features that make it a must-have for both novice cooks and seasoned chefs alike.

At its core, the Ninja Air Fryer Max XL employs advanced air frying technology, which circulates hot air around food to achieve that coveted crispy texture without the need for excessive oil. This method not only reduces the fat content of your meals but also enhances the natural flavours of your ingredients. Imagine enjoying your favourite fried dishes—crispy chips, succulent chicken wings, or even doughnuts—without the guilt that often accompanies deep frying. With the Ninja Air Fryer Max XL, you can indulge in healthier versions of classic comfort foods, allowing you to maintain a balanced diet without sacrificing taste.

One of the standout features of the Ninja Air Fryer Max XL is its generous capacity. With a 5.2-litre cooking basket, this appliance is ideal for preparing meals for families or gatherings. You can easily cook enough food to serve multiple people in one go, significantly reducing cooking time and effort. Whether you're hosting a dinner party or preparing a weeknight meal, the ample space allows you to fry, roast, bake, or dehydrate an array of dishes simultaneously.

Another impressive aspect of the Ninja Air Fryer Max XL is its versatility. It is designed to perform a multitude of cooking functions, making it a true multi-cooker. In addition to air frying, you can use it for roasting vegetables, baking cakes, dehydrating fruits, and even reheating leftovers. This multi-functionality not only saves space in your kitchen but also reduces the need for multiple appliances.

Imagine the convenience of having one machine that can tackle various cooking tasks, all while delivering consistent and delicious results.

The appliance features a user-friendly interface with an intuitive digital control panel, allowing you to easily select cooking functions, set temperatures, and adjust cooking times. The clear display ensures that you can monitor your cooking progress effortlessly. With a wide temperature range of 40°C to 210°C, the Ninja Air Fryer Max XL provides you with the flexibility to experiment with various recipes and cooking techniques. Whether you're looking to achieve the perfect golden-brown finish on your fries or slowly dehydrate fruits for a healthy snack, this air fryer has you covered.

Safety is a top priority in the design of the Ninja Air Fryer Max XL. The appliance is equipped with a range of safety features, including an automatic shut-off function that kicks in once the cooking time is complete. This ensures that your food is not only cooked to perfection but also prevents the risk of overcooking. Additionally, the exterior remains cool to the touch, reducing the risk of burns during operation. These thoughtful design elements make it a safe choice for families, providing peace of mind while you cook.

The air fryer has rapidly gained popularity in homes across the UK, and the Ninja Air Fryer Max XL exemplifies why. Its combination of health-conscious cooking, versatility, and ease of use make it an invaluable addition to any kitchen. Families can enjoy crispy, delicious meals with significantly less fat, while busy individuals can whip up quick, nutritious dishes without the fuss.

In conclusion, the Ninja Air Fryer Max XL is not merely a kitchen gadget; it is a revolutionary tool that redefines the way we cook. With its advanced air frying technology, ample cooking capacity, and multi-functionality, it stands out as a top choice for those looking to enhance their culinary skills while maintaining a healthier lifestyle. Embrace the future of cooking with the Ninja Air Fryer Max XL, and enjoy delicious, guilt-free meals that the whole family will love. Whether you are a busy professional, a home cook, or a culinary enthusiast, this appliance is sure to become a beloved staple in your kitchen, making every meal an occasion to celebrate.

Benefits of Using It

The Ninja Air Fryer Max XL has quickly become a favourite in kitchens across the UK, and it's not hard to see why. With its innovative technology and versatile functionality, this appliance offers a wealth of benefits that can enhance your cooking experience. Here are twelve compelling advantages of using the Ninja Air Fryer Max XL:

1. Healthier Cooking Options
One of the standout features of the Ninja Air Fryer Max XL is its ability to cook with significantly less oil compared to traditional frying methods. By using hot air circulation to achieve that crispy texture we all love, you can prepare your favourite fried foods with up to 75% less fat. This healthier approach to cooking allows you to enjoy delicious meals without the guilt often associated with deep-fried dishes, making it easier to maintain a balanced diet.

2. Versatility in Cooking Methods
The Ninja Air Fryer Max XL is not just an air fryer; it's a multi-functional cooking appliance that allows you to bake, roast, reheat, dehydrate, and even grill. This versatility means you can prepare a wide range of dishes, from crispy chips and chicken wings to perfectly baked cakes and dried fruits. The ability to perform multiple cooking methods in one appliance saves space and reduces the need for various kitchen gadgets.

3. Generous Capacity
With a 5.2-litre cooking basket, the Ninja Air Fryer Max XL is designed to cater to families and gatherings. This generous capacity

enables you to cook larger portions in a single batch, which is perfect for feeding multiple people. Whether you're preparing a family dinner or hosting a get-together, you can easily whip up enough food to satisfy everyone without having to cook in stages.

4. Quick Cooking Times

Time is often a constraint in our busy lives, and the Ninja Air Fryer Max XL helps alleviate this issue. Thanks to its advanced air frying technology, foods cook faster than in traditional ovens. Preheating is minimal, and cooking times are significantly reduced, allowing you to serve up delicious meals in a fraction of the time. This is particularly beneficial for weeknight dinners when you need to get food on the table quickly.

5. Crispy Texture Without Compromise

Achieving that perfect crispy texture is essential for many dishes, and the Ninja Air Fryer Max XL excels in this area. Its powerful heating elements and efficient air circulation create an ideal environment for achieving that sought-after crunch on the outside while keeping the inside tender and juicy. This means you can enjoy the same satisfying textures as deep-fried foods without the added grease.

6. User-Friendly Interface

The Ninja Air Fryer Max XL is designed with user experience in mind. The intuitive digital control panel makes it easy to select cooking functions, adjust temperatures, and set timers. With clearly marked buttons and a digital display, even novice cooks can operate the appliance with confidence. This simplicity encourages experimentation and creativity in the kitchen.

7. Safety Features

Safety is paramount in any kitchen, and the Ninja Air Fryer Max XL incorporates several safety features to give you peace of mind while cooking. The appliance is equipped with an automatic shut-off function, which activates once the cooking time is complete. Additionally, the exterior remains cool to the touch during operation, minimising the risk of burns. These thoughtful safety measures make it suitable for families and busy households.

8. Easy Cleaning and Maintenance

Post-cooking cleanup can often be a chore, but the Ninja Air Fryer Max XL makes it easier than ever. The non-stick cooking basket and crisper plate are dishwasher-safe, allowing for effortless cleaning. The smooth surfaces also wipe down easily, ensuring that your appliance stays in top condition. This hassle-free maintenance encourages more frequent use, as you won't dread the cleanup process.

9. Energy Efficiency

In an age where energy efficiency is more important than ever, the Ninja Air Fryer Max XL stands out as an economical choice. It uses less energy than conventional ovens, which is especially beneficial during the warmer months when you may not want to heat up your entire kitchen. Its quick cooking times also mean that you'll spend less time using electricity, contributing to lower energy bills.

10. Enhanced Flavour Profile

One of the advantages of using an air fryer is that it enhances the natural flavours of your ingredients. The Ninja Air Fryer Max XL locks in moisture while promoting caramelisation, resulting in dishes that are bursting with flavour. You can experiment with various herbs, spices, and marinades to create meals that are both nutritious and delicious, allowing your culinary creativity to shine.

11. Recipe Inspiration and Community

When you invest in a Ninja Air Fryer Max XL, you're not just getting an appliance; you're also gaining access to a vibrant community of fellow air fryer enthusiasts. The accompanying recipe book provides inspiration for dishes ranging from appetizers to desserts, encouraging you to explore new flavours and techniques. Additionally, numerous online forums and social media groups offer a platform to share recipes, tips, and tricks, enhancing your cooking journey.

12. Great for Meal Prep

With the Ninja Air Fryer Max XL, meal prep becomes a breeze. Its large capacity allows you to cook multiple portions at once, making it ideal for batch cooking. You can prepare healthy meals in advance, which is especially useful for busy weeks ahead. Portion your meals into containers, and you'll have convenient, nutritious options ready to go, saving both time and effort throughout the week.

The Ninja Air Fryer Max XL offers a wealth of benefits that make it a standout appliance in any kitchen. From healthier cooking options and versatile functionality to user-friendly features and quick cooking times, it enhances your culinary experience while promoting a balanced lifestyle. Whether you're cooking for yourself, your family, or entertaining guests, the Ninja Air Fryer Max XL is your go-to companion for delicious, satisfying meals that don't compromise on flavour or health. Embrace the future of cooking and transform your kitchen adventures with this remarkable appliance.

Before First Use

Before you start using your new appliance, you should ensure everything is ready to start your cooking.

1. Carefully remove and dispose of all packaging materials, promotional labels, and any tape that may be affixed to the unit. Ensuring that the appliance is free from any extraneous items will help you assess its condition and prepare it for use.

2. Take out all included accessories from the packaging and ensure that you read this manual thoroughly before operating the appliance. It is particularly important to pay close attention to the operational instructions, warnings, and essential safety precautions outlined within. This will help you avoid any potential injuries or damage to property while using the unit.

3. Wash the ceramic-coated basket, crisper plate, and all accessories in hot, soapy water. After cleaning, make sure to rinse them thoroughly to remove any soap residue, and then dry them completely with a soft cloth. It is crucial to note that you must NEVER clean the main unit in the dishwasher, as doing so could damage its components and impair functionality.

Step-By-Step Using It

This is a 7-in-1 versatility appliance meaning you can max crisp, air fry, air roast, air broil, bake, reheat, and dehydrate. Here's how to use each function.

Max Crisp

Steps:

1. Prepare the Crisper Plate:
Begin by placing the crisper plate securely in the cooking basket. This plate is designed to elevate the food, allowing for optimal air circulation and achieving that desired crispy texture.

2. Select the Max Crisp Function:
Press the MAX CRISP button. The default temperature setting

will be displayed on the control panel. It's important to note that the temperature cannot be adjusted while using the Max Crisp function, as it is optimised for maximum crispiness.

3. Set the Cooking Time:
Use the TIME up and down arrow buttons to adjust the cooking time according to your recipe. This allows you to tailor the cooking duration to ensure your ingredients are perfectly cooked.

4. Add Ingredients:
Carefully place your ingredients into the basket, ensuring they are evenly spread out for uniform cooking. Once the ingredients are added, insert the basket back into the main unit.

5. Start the Cooking Process:
Press the START/STOP button to initiate cooking. The appliance will begin to circulate hot air around the ingredients, creating that crispy finish.

6. Tossing Ingredients:
If you wish to toss or shake the ingredients during the cooking process, simply remove the basket from the unit. This action will automatically pause the cooking timer. Shake the basket gently back and forth to redistribute the ingredients for even cooking. Once you have finished, reinsert the basket into the unit, and cooking will automatically resume.

7. Completion Notification:
When the cooking time is complete, the appliance will beep to alert you, and the word End will appear on the control panel display, indicating that your food is ready.

8. Removing Cooked Ingredients:
Carefully remove the ingredients from the basket. You can either dump them out directly into a serving dish or use oven mitts or silicone-tipped tongs to safely handle the hot basket and food. This ensures you avoid burns and enjoy your perfectly cooked dish without hassle.

Air Fry

Steps:

1. Prepare the Basket:
Before you begin, ensure that the air fryer basket is thoroughly clean and completely dry. This is crucial for optimal cooking results. Next, place the crisper plate securely within the basket. This plate helps elevate the food, allowing for better air circulation during the cooking process.

2. Grease the Basket:
Lightly grease the air fryer basket with a small amount of oil to help prevent sticking and enhance crispiness. Alternatively, you may opt to use parchment liners specifically designed for air fryers. These liners can provide an additional layer of convenience and ensure easier cleanup.

3. Add Ingredients:
Carefully add your ingredients to the basket, ensuring that they are spread out evenly. Avoid overcrowding the basket, as this can hinder proper air circulation and result in uneven cooking. It's best to leave some space between items to achieve that perfect crispiness.

4. Select the Air Fry Function:
Press the AIR FRY button or function to activate this cooking mode. The control panel will display the default temperature setting. You can adjust the temperature and cooking time according to your recipe by using the TEMP up and down arrows, as well as the TIME up and down buttons. This allows you to tailor the cooking process to suit your specific ingredients.

5. Insert the Basket:
Once you have set the desired temperature and time, ensure that the ingredients are properly positioned on the crisper plate. Then, carefully place the basket into the air fryer unit, ensuring it is securely locked in place.

6. Start Cooking:
Press the START/STOP button to begin the cooking process. The appliance will commence air circulation, cooking your ingredients to perfection.

7. Completion Notification:
Upon the completion of the cooking cycle, you will hear a beep sound, and the word END will appear on the control panel display. This indicates that your food is ready to be enjoyed.

8. Remove the Basket:
Put on heat-resistant gloves to protect your hands from the heat. Carefully remove the basket from the unit, ensuring that you handle it safely. Transfer the cooked ingredients onto serving plates, and enjoy your deliciously air-fried meal!

Air Roast

Steps:

1. Prepare the Crisper Plate:
If required, place the crisper plate in the basket. However, note that the crisper plate is not necessary when using a baking dish. If you are opting for a baking dish, ensure it fits comfortably within the basket.

2. Select the Air Roast Function:
Press the AIR ROAST button to activate this cooking mode. The default time and temperature settings will automatically appear on the control panel. Feel free to adjust both the time and temperature to suit your specific recipe and desired cooking results.

3. Prepare Your Ingredients:
Lightly grease your ingredients to enhance flavour and prevent sticking. Once prepared, place them in the basket, ensuring they are arranged evenly for optimal roasting. If using a baking dish, place the greased ingredients directly in the dish instead.

4. Start the Cooking Process:
After you've set the desired time and temperature, press the START/STOP button to begin cooking. The appliance will start circulating hot air around the ingredients, ensuring even cooking and browning.

5. Completion Notification:
When the cooking time is complete, you will hear a beep sound, and the word END will appear on the display. This indicates that your food is ready to be removed.

6. Serve Your Food:
Carefully remove the basket from the unit. Use oven mitts to protect your hands from the heat. Serve the roasted food directly from the basket or transfer it to serving plates. Enjoy your perfectly air-roasted meal!

Air Broil

Steps:

1. Prepare the Crisper Plate:
Begin by installing the crisper plate in the basket. This component is essential for ensuring that your food is elevated, allowing hot air to circulate evenly during the broiling process.

2. Select the Air Broil Function:
Press the AIR BROIL button to activate this cooking mode. The default temperature setting will be displayed on the control panel. You can adjust the temperature to your preference using the TEMP up and down arrow buttons, ensuring it aligns with your recipe requirements.

3. Set the Cooking Time:
Next, use the TIME up and down arrow buttons to set the desired cooking duration. This flexibility allows you to tailor the cooking time to achieve your preferred level of doneness.

4. Add Ingredients:
Carefully add your ingredients to the basket, ensuring they are spread out evenly for optimal cooking. Once you have arranged the food, insert the basket back into the unit, making sure it is securely in place.

5. Start Cooking:
Press the START/STOP button to commence the cooking process. The appliance will begin circulating hot air, effectively broiling your ingredients to achieve a beautifully browned exterior.

6. Completion Notification:
When the cooking time is up, the unit will beep to signal that the process is complete, and the word END will appear on the control panel display. This indicates that your food is ready to be removed.

7. Remove Ingredients:
To safely retrieve your cooked food, you can either dump the ingredients out of the basket or use oven mitts or silicone-tipped tongs to handle the hot basket and food. This ensures safe serving while preserving the deliciousness of your broiled dish. Enjoy your meal!

Bake

Steps:

1. Prepare the Crisper Plate:
If necessary, install the crisper plate in the basket. However, if you are using a baking dish, the crisper plate is not required. Ensure that the baking dish fits comfortably within the basket.

2. Select the Bake Function:
Press the BAKE button to activate this cooking mode. The default temperature setting will appear on the control panel. Adjust the temperature to your desired level by using the TEMP up and down arrow buttons, allowing you to tailor the cooking conditions to your specific recipe.

3. Set the Cooking Time:
Use the TIME up and down arrow buttons to set the cooking duration according to your recipe's requirements. This gives you control over how long your dish will be baking, ensuring optimal results.

4. Add Ingredients:
Carefully place your ingredients into the basket, ensuring they are evenly distributed for consistent cooking. Once you've arranged the food, insert the basket back into the unit, making sure it is securely positioned.

5. Start the Cooking Process:
Press the START/STOP button to begin the baking process. The appliance will circulate hot air around the ingredients, providing an even bake.

6. Completion Notification:
Once the cooking time has elapsed, the unit will emit a beep to indicate that the baking process is complete, and the word END will be displayed on the control panel. This alerts you that your dish is ready to be removed.

7. Remove Ingredients:
To retrieve your baked goods, you can either dump the ingredients out of the basket or use oven mitts or silicone-tipped tongs to handle the hot basket safely. This ensures a safe and convenient serving experience, allowing you to enjoy your deliciously baked dish!

Reheat

Steps:

1. Prepare the Crisper Plate:
Begin by placing the crisper plate in the basket. This component helps ensure that your food heats evenly, preventing it from becoming soggy.

2. Select the Reheat Function:
Press the REHEAT button to activate this cooking mode. The default temperature and time settings will automatically appear on the control panel. You can adjust these settings as needed to suit your specific ingredients or preferences.

3. Add Ingredients:
Carefully add your leftovers or any food items that need reheating to the basket. Ensure that they are arranged evenly to promote even heating. Once you've added the ingredients, set the basket securely back into the unit.

4. Start the Cooking Process:
Press the START/STOP button to begin reheating. The appliance will circulate hot air around the food, warming it thoroughly while helping to maintain its original texture.

5. Completion Notification:
When the reheating process is complete, you will hear a beep sound, and the word END will appear on the display. This indicates that your food is ready to be served.

6. Serve the Food:
Carefully remove the basket from the unit, taking care to avoid burns. You can then transfer the reheated food onto serving plates. Enjoy your meal, freshly warmed to perfection!

Dehydrate

Steps:

1. Prepare Your Ingredients:
Begin by slicing your ingredients into uniform pieces. This ensures even drying and helps achieve the desired texture. Depending on what you're dehydrating, you may want to consider the thickness of each slice for optimal results.

2. Layer the Ingredients:
Place the first layer of sliced ingredients at the bottom of the basket. Then, position the crisper plate on top of this layer to create a barrier. Next, add a second layer of ingredients on top of the crisper plate. This method promotes proper air circulation and prevents the ingredients from sticking together.

3. Transfer the Basket:
Once your layers are set, carefully transfer the basket into the unit, ensuring it is securely in place.

4. Select the Dehydrate Function:
Press the DEHYDRATE button to activate this cooking mode. The default temperature and time settings will appear on the control panel. Adjust these settings according to your specific recipe or the type of ingredients you are dehydrating, as different foods require varying temperatures and times.

5. Start the Cooking Process:
Press the START/STOP button to initiate the dehydrating process. The appliance will circulate hot air, effectively removing moisture from the ingredients while preserving their flavour and nutrients.

6. Completion Notification:
When the dehydrating process is complete, a beep sound will signal that it is done, and the word END will appear on the display. This indicates that your dehydrated snacks or ingredients are ready for use.

7. Remove and Enjoy:
Carefully remove the basket from the unit, taking care to avoid burns. Allow the dehydrated items to cool before storing or enjoying them as healthy snacks!

Tips for Using Accessories

The Ninja Air Fryer Max XL comes with a range of accessories designed to enhance your cooking experience. Proper use of these accessories can elevate your meals and streamline your cooking

process. Here are some helpful tips to maximise their potential:

1. Baking Dish:
If you're using a baking dish, ensure it fits comfortably within the basket. Lightly grease the dish or use parchment paper to prevent sticking. This is particularly useful when baking cakes or casseroles. Always check the manufacturer's recommendations for temperature limits to avoid damaging the dish.

2. Silicone Moulds:
Silicone moulds are great for making treats like muffins or desserts. They are non-stick and flexible, making it easy to remove your baked goods without damage. Be sure to place them on the crisper plate or a heat-resistant surface within the basket for even cooking.

3. Skewers:
If you're using skewers, ensure they are appropriately sized for the basket. Alternate between meat and vegetables for balanced cooking. Remember to soak wooden skewers in water for about 30 minutes before use to prevent burning.

4. Use Parchment Liners:
Parchment liners can make cleanup easier and prevent food from sticking to the basket. Choose perforated liners designed for air fryers to allow proper airflow. This can be particularly beneficial for messy foods like marinated meats.

Cleaning and Caring for the Ninja Air Fryer Max XL

Maintaining your Ninja Air Fryer Max XL is essential for ensuring its longevity and optimal performance. Regular cleaning not only enhances the cooking quality but also helps prevent any build-up of grease and food particles that could affect the flavour of your meals. Here's a comprehensive guide on how to clean and care for your air fryer effectively.

1. Unplug and Cool Down:
Before cleaning, always unplug the appliance and allow it to cool completely. This prevents burns and makes handling the parts safer.

2. Disassemble the Components:
Remove the cooking basket, crisper plate, and any other accessories from the unit. This makes it easier to clean each part thoroughly.

3. Hand Washing:
Wash the basket, crisper plate, and other accessories in warm, soapy water. Use a soft sponge or cloth to avoid scratching the non-stick surfaces. For stubborn residue, soak the items in hot, soapy water for a while before scrubbing. Rinse thoroughly to remove any soap residue.

4. Dishwasher Safe Parts:
Some components are dishwasher safe. Refer to the user manual to check which parts can be placed in the dishwasher. If using a dishwasher, place the items on the top rack to prevent damage.

5. Clean the Main Unit:
Wipe down the exterior of the air fryer with a damp cloth. Avoid using abrasive cleaners or scouring pads, as they can damage the finish. For the interior, a damp cloth can be used to remove any splatters or grease. Ensure that no moisture enters the heating element or electrical components.

6. Regular Maintenance:
To maintain peak performance, regularly inspect the appliance for any signs of wear or damage. Check the power cord for frays and ensure that all components fit snugly together.

7. Odour Removal:
If you notice any lingering odours, you can place a bowl of water mixed with lemon juice inside the basket and run the air fryer for a few minutes. This will help neutralise any unpleasant smells.

Fundamentals of Ninja Air Fryer Max XL

8. Store Properly:
When not in use, store the air fryer in a cool, dry place. Ensure that the basket and other components are clean and dry before storing to prevent mould or odour buildup.

By following these cleaning and care tips, you can ensure that your Ninja Air Fryer Max XL remains in excellent condition, providing you with delicious, healthy meals for years to come. Regular maintenance is key to enjoying the full benefits of this versatile kitchen appliance.

Frequently Asked Questions & Notes

1. Is it safe to leave the Ninja Air Fryer Max XL unattended while cooking?
While the Ninja Air Fryer Max XL is designed with safety features, such as automatic shut-off and overheat protection, it's best practice to stay nearby while it's in use. This allows you to monitor the cooking process, check on the food, and respond quickly if needed. If you're trying a new recipe or cooking unfamiliar foods, keeping an eye on the air fryer can help ensure the best results and prevent any potential issues.

2. Can I use oil when cooking in the air fryer?
Yes, while the air fryer is designed to cook with minimal oil, adding a light coat can enhance flavour and crispiness. It's advisable to use oil with a high smoke point, such as avocado or vegetable oil, for best results.

3. Is it possible to cook frozen foods directly in the air fryer?
Absolutely! The Ninja Air Fryer Max XL is excellent for cooking frozen foods straight from the freezer. Just remember to adjust the cooking time accordingly, as frozen items may require a few extra minutes compared to fresh ingredients.

4. How do I clean the air fryer?
Cleaning is straightforward. The basket and crisper plate are removable and can be washed in warm, soapy water or placed in the dishwasher. Wipe down the main unit with a damp cloth. Always allow the appliance to cool before cleaning.

5. Can I bake in the Ninja Air Fryer Max XL?
Yes, this versatile appliance allows you to bake, roast, and even dehydrate foods. You can use various accessories, such as baking dishes and silicone moulds, to expand your cooking options.

6. What types of food can I cook?
The Ninja Air Fryer Max XL can handle a wide variety of foods, including meats, vegetables, baked goods, and even snacks like chips. It's perfect for experimenting with different recipes and cooking techniques.

7. Is it safe to use the air fryer in a small kitchen?
Yes, the Ninja Air Fryer Max XL is compact and designed to fit comfortably on countertops. Just ensure there's adequate ventilation around the appliance while in use to maintain safety.

8. What should I do if my air fryer starts smoking?
If your air fryer begins to smoke, it could be due to excess oil or food residue. Turn off the appliance, unplug it, and allow it to cool. Clean the basket and crisper plate thoroughly before using it again.

4-Week Meal Plan

Week 1

Day 1:
Breakfast: Cheesy Bacon Egg Muffins
Lunch: Air Fried Vegetable Skewers
Snack: Broccoli Cheddar Casserole
Dinner: Cajun Chicken Breasts
Dessert: Yummy Black 'n' White Brownies

Day 2:
Breakfast: Cheese and Sausage Quiche
Lunch: Tasty Cheese Spinach Frittata
Snack: Fluffy Cloud Eggs
Dinner: Crispy Fish with Potato Wedges
Dessert: Orange Polenta Cake

Day 3:
Breakfast: Bacon and Eggs Breakfast
Lunch: Crispy Turnip Fries
Snack: Crispy Flax Cheddar Cheese Chips
Dinner: Beef and Sausage Meatballs
Dessert: Chocolate Chip Cookies

Day 4:
Breakfast: Flavourful Cheese Onion Risotto
Lunch: Tomato Avocado Boats
Snack: Bacon-Wrapped Sausage
Dinner: Spicy Chicken Wings
Dessert: Sweet Banana Cake

Day 5:
Breakfast: Baked Pecan French Toast
Lunch: Cauliflower Pizza Crust
Snack: Crispy Mozzarella Cheese Sticks
Dinner: Garlic Prawns with Pasta Alfredo
Dessert: Chocolate Chip Macadamia Nut Cookies

Day 6:
Breakfast: Cheese Tomato Frittata
Lunch: Cheese Soufflés with Mushrooms
Snack: Garlicky Radish Chips
Dinner: Classic Meatloaf
Dessert: Coconut Cream Cheese Muffins

Day 7:
Breakfast: Apple Pancakes
Lunch: Courgette Fritters
Snack: Buffalo Cauliflower Florets
Dinner: Kofta Kebabs
Dessert: Chocolate Soufflé

Week 2

Day 1:
Breakfast: Scrambled Eggs with Mushrooms
Lunch: Homemade Roasted Brussels Sprouts with Bacon
Snack: Roasted Taco Cauliflower
Dinner: Cheesy Chicken and Courgette Casserole
Dessert: Mini Chocolate Cake

Day 2:
Breakfast: Spinach and Cheese Quiche
Lunch: Simple Courgette Ribbons
Snack: Cheese Drop Biscuits
Dinner: Lemon Salmon Skewers
Dessert: Easy Peanut Butter Cookies

Day 3:
Breakfast: Sweet Cranberry Muffins
Lunch: Garlic Broccoli with Sriracha
Snack: Rosemary Potato Chips with Sour Cream
Dinner: Low-Carb Lasagna
Dessert: Vanilla Butter Cake

Day 4:
Breakfast: Fluffy Corn Bread
Lunch: Prosciutto-Wrapped Asparagus
Snack: Cheesy Cauliflower Bites
Dinner: Almond-Crusted Chicken Nuggets
Dessert: Yummy Black 'n' White Brownies

Day 5:
Breakfast: Homemade Pork Patties
Lunch: Healthy Tamari Green Beans
Snack: Balsamic Roasted Brussels Sprouts
Dinner: Crispy Fried Prawns
Dessert: Orange Polenta Cake

Day 6:
Breakfast: Air Fried Scotch Eggs
Lunch: Garlic Roasted Cherry Tomatoes
Snack: Crunchy Spanish Peanuts
Dinner: Ham Mac 'N' Cheese
Dessert: Chocolate Chip Cookies

Day 7:
Breakfast: Cheesy Egg Stuffed Peppers
Lunch: Air Fried Vegetable Skewers
Snack: Pigs in a Blanket
Dinner: Air Fried Short Ribs
Dessert: Coconut Cream Cheese Muffins

Week 3

Day 1:
Breakfast: Nut and Berry Granola
Lunch: Roasted Brussels Sprouts
Snack: Shakshuka Harissa
Dinner: Crispy Popcorn Chicken
Dessert: Sweet Banana Cake

Day 2:
Breakfast: Glazed Ham Steak
Lunch: Tomato Avocado Boats
Snack: Tasty Masala Omelet
Dinner: Salmon with Coconut Avocado Sauce
Dessert: Chocolate Chip Macadamia Nut Cookies

Day 3:
Breakfast: Cheesy Bacon Egg Muffins
Lunch: Cauliflower Pizza Crust
Snack: Fluffy Cloud Eggs
Dinner: Homemade Cheeseburgers
Dessert: Chocolate Soufflé

Day 4:
Breakfast: Bacon and Eggs Breakfast
Lunch: Cheese Soufflés with Mushrooms
Snack: Crispy Flax Cheddar Cheese Chips
Dinner: Turkey Breasts with Shallot
Dessert: Mini Chocolate Cake

Day 5:
Breakfast: Cheese and Sausage Quiche
Lunch: Courgette Fritters
Snack: Bacon-Wrapped Sausage
Dinner: Tender Garlic Cod Fish
Dessert: Easy Peanut Butter Cookies

Day 6:
Breakfast: Flavourful Cheese Onion Risotto
Lunch: Homemade Roasted Brussels Sprouts with Bacon
Snack: Garlicky Radish Chips
Dinner: Authentic Carne Asada
Dessert: Vanilla Butter Cake

Day 7:
Breakfast: Baked Pecan French Toast
Lunch: Prosciutto-Wrapped Asparagus
Snack: Crispy Mozzarella Cheese Sticks
Dinner: Crispy Parmesan Pork Chops
Dessert: Yummy Black 'n' White Brownies

Week 4

Day 1:
Breakfast: Spinach and Cheese Quiche
Lunch: Simple Courgette Ribbons
Snack: Buffalo Cauliflower Florets
Dinner: Air Fryer Crispy Whole Chicken Wings
Dessert: Orange Polenta Cake

Day 2:
Breakfast: Sweet Cranberry Muffins
Lunch: Garlic Broccoli with Sriracha
Snack: Rosemary Potato Chips with Sour Cream
Dinner: Pesto Fish Finger Burgers
Dessert: Chocolate Chip Cookies

Day 3:
Breakfast: Apple Pancakes
Lunch: Healthy Tamari Green Beans
Snack: Balsamic Roasted Brussels Sprouts
Dinner: Lamb Patties with Feta
Dessert: Sweet Banana Cake

Day 4:
Breakfast: Cheese Tomato Frittata
Lunch: Roasted Brussels Sprouts
Snack: Cheesy Cauliflower Bites
Dinner: Buttermilk Fried Chicken Breasts
Dessert: Chocolate Chip Macadamia Nut Cookies

Day 5:
Breakfast: Scrambled Eggs with Mushrooms
Lunch: Garlic Roasted Cherry Tomatoes
Snack: Cheese Drop Biscuits
Dinner: Garlic Butter Lobster Tails
Dessert: Coconut Cream Cheese Muffins

Day 6:
Breakfast: Fluffy Corn Bread
Lunch: Tomato Avocado Boats
Snack: Crunchy Spanish Peanuts
Dinner: Perfect Beef Roast
Dessert: Chocolate Soufflé

Day 7:
Breakfast: Homemade Pork Patties
Lunch: Cauliflower Pizza Crust
Snack: Pigs in a Blanket
Dinner: Juicy Garlic Butter Steak
Dessert: Easy Peanut Butter Cookies

Chapter 1 Breakfast

Cheesy Bacon Egg Muffins

⏲ Prep: 10 minutes 🍳 Cook: 20 minutes 🍽 Serves: 2

1 tablespoon green pesto
75g shredded cheese
150g cooked bacon
1 spring onion, chopped
2 eggs

1. Select Air Fry mode, and set the cooking temperature at 180°C and adjust the cooking time to 20 minutes. Let the Ninja Air Fryer Max preheat for 3 minutes. 2. Place liners in a regular cupcake tin. 3. Beat the eggs with pepper, salt, and the pesto in a bowl. Mix in the cheese. 4. Pour the eggs into the cupcake tin and top with the bacon and spring onion. 5. Cook them for 15-20 minutes until the egg is set.
Per Serving: Calories 691; Fat 53.23g; Sodium 2057mg; Carbs 10.37g; Fibre 2.2g; Sugar 3.82g; Protein 44.85g

Bacon and Eggs Breakfast

⏲ Prep: 5 minutes 🍳 Cook: 5 minutes 🍽 Serves: 1

Parsley
5 cherry tomatoes
150g bacon
2 eggs

1. Select Air Fry mode, and set the cooking temperature at 180°C and adjust the cooking time to 5 minutes. Let the Ninja Air Fryer Max preheat for 3 minutes. 2. Once preheated, air-fry the bacon for 5 minutes or until done; take out the bacon and then cook the eggs in the Ninja Air Fryer Max for 5 minutes with some pepper and salt on them. 3. Serve the dish, sprinkle them with some parsley and enjoy with the cherry tomatoes on the side.
Per Serving: Calories 286; Fat 19.46g; Sodium 210mg; Carbs 8.7g; Fibre 0.9g; Sugar 6.57g; Protein 18.44g

Cheese and Sausage Quiche

⏰ **Prep:** 10 minutes 🍲 **Cook:** 25 minutes 📚 **Serves:** 4

12 large eggs
240g heavy cream
1 teaspoon black pepper
300g sausage
200g shredded cheddar cheese

1. Install the crisper plate in the basket. 2. Select Bake mode, and set the cooking temperature at 190°C and adjust the cooking time to 25 minutes. Let the Ninja Air Fryer Max preheat for 3 minutes. 3. Whisk the eggs, heavy cream and pepper in a heatproof bowl; add in the sausage and cheddar cheese. 4. Bake the mixture for 25 minutes. 5. Serve hot.
Per Serving: Calories 286; Fat 19.46g; Sodium 210mg; Carbs 8.7g; Fibre 0.9g; Sugar 6.57g; Protein 18.44g

Spinach and Cheese Quiche

⏰ **Prep:** 20 minutes 🍲 **Cook:** 30 minutes 📚 **Serves:** 2

3 whole eggs
75g cottage cheese
100g chopped spinach
25g parmesan cheese
60ml of milk

1. Select Bake mode, and set the cooking temperature at 180°C and adjust the cooking time to 45 minutes. Let the Ninja Air Fryer Max preheat for 3 minutes. 2. In a heatproof bowl, whisk the eggs, cottage cheese, parmesan, and milk and transfer the mixture to a baking pan that fits your air fryer. Mix in the spinach and then sprinkle the cheese on top. 3. Place the baking pan in the air fryer. 4. Bake the food for 25-30 minutes. 5. Let the dish cool for 5 minutes and serve.
Per Serving: Calories 219; Fat 12.78g; Sodium 526mg; Carbs 6.91g; Fibre 1.1g; Sugar 3.14g; Protein 18.95g

Flavourful Cheese Onion Risotto

⏲ **Prep: 15 minutes**   🍲 **Cook: 26 minutes**   📚 **Serves: 2**

1 onion, diced
480ml chicken stock, boiling
50g parmesan or cheddar cheese, grated
1 clove garlic, minced
150g Arborio rice
1 tablespoon olive oil
1 tablespoon unsalted butter

1. Install the crisper plate in the basket. 2. Select Air Fry mode, and set the cooking temperature at 200°C and adjust the cooking time to 45 minutes. Let the Ninja Air Fryer Max preheat for 3 minutes. 3. Grease a round baking tin, small enough to fit inside the fryer, and stir in the garlic, butter, and onion. 4. Transfer the tin to the basket and cook them for 4 minutes. Add in the rice and cook for a further 4 minutes, giving it a stir three times throughout the cooking time. 5. Adjust the cooking temperature to 160°C and add in the chicken stock, before gently mixing it. Leave them to cook for 22 minutes with the fryer uncovered. 6. Before serving, throw in the cheese and give it one more stir. Enjoy!

Per Serving: Calories 379; Fat 27.38g; Sodium 1382mg; Carbs 32.19g; Fibre 10.3g; Sugar 3.83g; Protein 15.54g

Baked Pecan French Toast

⏲ **Prep: 15 minutes**   🍲 **Cook: 10 minutes**   📚 **Serves: 4**

2 large eggs
160ml whole milk
1 teaspoon vanilla
4 slices French bread
75g brown sugar
55g butter
110g chopped pecans
¼ teaspoon cinnamon

1. Install the crisper plate in the basket. 2. Select Bake mode, and set the cooking temperature at 180°C and adjust the cooking time to 10 minutes. Let the Ninja Air Fryer Max preheat for 3 minutes. 3. In a suitable bowl, stir together the eggs, milk, and vanilla until smooth. 4. Place the French bread slices into the bowl and let sit for 1 minute. Then turn the bread and let sit until you're ready to cook. 5. Add the brown sugar and butter to a small saucepan and melt them over low heat with stirring them occasionally. 6. In a small bowl, toss the pecans with the cinnamon. 7. Line the crisper plate with parchment paper, and then transfer the bread from the egg mixture to it; drizzle the brown sugar mixture over the bread and top with the pecans. 8. Bake the food for 7 to 9 minutes or until the French toast is golden brown and crisp. Serve.

Per Serving: Calories 731; Fat 30.33g; Sodium 955mg; Carbs 98.08g; Fibre 4.7g; Sugar 30.13g; Protein 19.17g

Cheese Tomato Frittata

⏲ **Prep: 15 minutes**　🍳 **Cook: 15 minutes**　🍽 **Serves: 3**

1 tablespoon unsalted butter, at room temperature
4 large eggs, beaten
60g ricotta cheese
60ml whole milk
1 teaspoon dried Italian seasoning
Pinch sea salt
2 spring onions, chopped
1 garlic clove, minced
50g chopped cherry tomatoes, drained
50g shredded provolone cheese
25g grated Parmesan cheese

1. Select Bake mode, and set the cooking temperature at 180°C and adjust the cooking time to 15 minutes. Let the Ninja Air Fryer Max preheat for 3 minutes. 2. Grease a suitable baking pan with the butter and set aside. 3. In a medium bowl, beat the eggs with the ricotta, milk, Italian seasoning, and salt. Pour this into the prepared pan. 4. Arrange the spring onions, garlic, and tomatoes on the eggs. Top them with the cheeses. 5. Cook them for 12 to 15 minutes or until the eggs are set and puffed. 6. Serve.

Per Serving: Calories 272; Fat 20.1g; Sodium 505mg; Carbs 7.56g; Fibre 0.4g; Sugar 3.49g; Protein 14.97g

Sweet Cranberry Muffins

⏲ **Prep: 15 minutes**　🍳 **Cook: 15 minutes**　🍽 **Serves: 4**

65g plain flour
2 tablespoons whole-wheat flour
½ teaspoon baking powder
2 tablespoons brown sugar
3 tablespoons quick-cooking oats
Pinch sea salt
1 large egg
60ml whole milk
1 teaspoon vanilla
2 tablespoons vegetable oil
35g dried cranberries
Nonstick baking spray containing flour

1. Install the crisper plate in the basket. 2. Select Bake mode, and set the cooking temperature at 160°C and adjust the cooking time to 15 minutes. Let the Ninja Air Fryer Max preheat for 3 minutes. 3. In a medium bowl, combine the plain and whole-wheat flours, baking powder, brown sugar, oats, and salt and mix. 4. In a small bowl or a measuring cup, beat together the egg, milk, vanilla, and oil until combined. 5. Add the egg mixture to the dry ingredients and stir them just until combined. Stir in the cranberries. 6. Spray four silicone muffin cups with the baking spray. Divide the batter among them, filling each two-thirds full. 7. Place the muffin cups in the Ninja Air Fryer Max basket; bake the food for 12 to 14 minutes until the muffins are browned and the tops spring back when you touch them lightly with your finger. 8. Allow the muffins to cool on a wire rack for 10 to 15 minutes before serving.

Per Serving: Calories 192; Fat 8.76g; Sodium 49mg; Carbs 25.16g; Fibre 1.1g; Sugar 8.59g; Protein 3.57g

Apple Pancakes

⏰ **Prep: 15 minutes**   🍳 **Cook: 15 minutes**   📚 **Serves: 3**

30g plain flour
1 tablespoon granulated sugar
¼ teaspoon baking powder
2 large eggs
60ml low fat milk
60g small curd cottage cheese
2 tablespoons vegetable oil
2 tablespoons butter
2 tablespoons brown sugar
1 Granny Smith apple, peeled, cored, and sliced ½cm thick
½ teaspoon cinnamon

1. Select Bake mode, and set the cooking temperature at 190°C and adjust the cooking time to 15 minutes. Let the Ninja Air Fryer Max preheat for 3 minutes. 2. In a medium bowl, combine the flour, baking powder, and sugar. 3. Whisk the eggs, milk, cottage cheese, and oil in another bowl until blended. 4. Add the egg mixture into the flour mixture and stir just until combined. Let stand while you prepare the apple mixture. 5. Put the butter in a suitable round pan and place the pan in the Ninja Air Fryer Max basket; cook for 1 minute and remove. 6. Swirl the pan so the butter coats the bottom and 1cm up the sides. Top them evenly with the brown sugar and apples, and sprinkle with the cinnamon. 7. Bake this mixture for 3 minutes or until the butter bubbles. Remove the pan. 8. Pour the batter over the apples. Return the pan to the Ninja Air Fryer Max and bake for 9 to 11 minutes or until the batter is golden brown. 9. Cut into three wedges to serve.
Per Serving: Calories 317; Fat 21.39g; Sodium 140mg; Carbs 26.05g; Fibre 2.1g; Sugar 14.76g; Protein 5.8g

Scrambled Eggs with Mushrooms

⏰ **Prep: 15 minutes**   🍳 **Cook: 16 minutes**   📚 **Serves: 3**

2 tablespoons butter
65g sliced mushrooms
1 spring onion, chopped
6 large eggs
2 tablespoons light cream
½ teaspoon dried thyme
½ teaspoon sea salt
⅛ teaspoon freshly ground black pepper

1. Select Bake mode, and set the cooking temperature at 180°C and adjust the cooking time to 15 minutes. Let the Ninja Air Fryer Max preheat for 3 minutes. 2. Place the butter in a suitable round pan and put the pan in the Ninja Air Fryer Max basket. Melt the butter in the Ninja Air Fryer Max for 1 minute. 3. Remove the pan and add the mushrooms and spring onion s to the pan. 4. Return the basket to the Ninja Air Fryer Max and bake for 5 minutes or until the mushrooms are lightly browned, shaking the pan after 3 minutes. Then remove to a serving plate and set aside. 5. In a medium bowl, whisk together the light cream, eggs, thyme, salt, and pepper until combined. 6. Pour the egg mixture into the pan and then bake them for 8 to 10 minutes, stirring the egg mixture gently after 5 minutes, until the eggs are set. 7. Serve warm.
Per Serving: Calories 199; Fat 18.65g; Sodium 470mg; Carbs 2.1g; Fibre 0.2g; Sugar 0.71g; Protein 5.89g

Fluffy Corn Bread

⏰ **Prep: 15 minutes**   🍲 **Cook: 22 minutes**   📚 **Serves: 4**

Nonstick baking spray containing flour
105g polenta
65g plain flour
1 teaspoon baking powder
½ teaspoon baking soda
¼ teaspoon sea salt
50g shredded Cheddar cheese
240ml buttermilk
2 large eggs
55g butter, melted
1 tablespoon honey

1. Select Bake mode, and set the cooking temperature at 180°C and adjust the cooking time to 25 minutes. Let the Ninja Air Fryer Max preheat for 3 minutes. 2. Spray a suitable round pan with the baking spray and set aside. 3. Combine the polenta, flour, baking powder, baking soda, and salt in a medium bowl. Add the cheese and toss to coat. 4. In a glass measuring cup, combine the buttermilk, butter, eggs, and honey until smooth. Add this mixture to the flour mixture and stir just until combined. 5. Lay out the batter on the prepared pan. 6. Bake the food for 17 to 22 minutes or until the corn bread is golden brown and a toothpick inserted in the centre comes out clean. 7. Let cool on a wire rack for 15 minutes before cutting into four wedges to serve.

Per Serving: Calories 392; Fat 20.51g; Sodium 624mg; Carbs 41.2g; Fibre 1.5g; Sugar 7.81g; Protein 10.96g

Homemade Pork Patties

⏰ **Prep: 15 minutes**   🍲 **Cook: 20 minutes**   **Serves: 4**

455g pork mince
1 teaspoon salt
1 teaspoon freshly ground black pepper
¾ teaspoon garlic powder
½ teaspoon ground sage
¼ teaspoon ground thyme
¼ teaspoon ground red pepper flakes

1. Install the crisper plate in the basket. 2. Select Air Fry mode, and set the cooking temperature at 200°C and adjust the cooking time to 20 minutes. Let the Ninja Air Fryer Max preheat. 3. In a large bowl, combine the pork, black pepper, salt, garlic powder, sage, thyme, and red pepper flakes. Mix the seasonings evenly into the pork. Avoid overworking the meat. 4. Divide the seasoned pork into ¼-cup portions, roll each portion into a ball, and press it down slightly to form a patty. 5. Place the patties in a single layer on the crisper plate, leaving a little space between each to ensure even cooking. 6. Air-fry for 10 minutes. 7. Flip the patties and air fry for an additional 5 to 8 minutes, or until the pork reaches an internal temperature of 70°C.

Per Serving: Calories 303; Fat 24.07g; Sodium 646mg; Carbs 1.13g; Fibre 0.3g; Sugar 0.16g; Protein 19.37g

Air Fried Scotch Eggs

⏰ Prep: 20 minutes   🍲 Cook: 10 minutes   ⬚ Serves: 4

455g pork sausage
1 tablespoon finely chopped chives
1 teaspoon dried minced onion
½ teaspoon salt
½ teaspoon freshly ground black pepper
30g plain flour
1 large egg
75g panko bread crumbs
4 hard-boiled eggs
Extra-virgin olive oil, for spraying

1. Install the crisper plate in the basket. 2. Select Air Fry mode, and set the cooking temperature at 200°C and adjust the cooking time to 10 minutes. Let the Ninja Air Fryer Max preheat. 3. In a medium bowl, combine the sausage, onion, salt, chives, and pepper. Gently mix until well combined. Shape the mixture into 4 equal-size patties. 4. Add the flour to a small shallow bowl. 5. Beat the egg in a second small shallow bowl. 6. Add the bread crumbs to a third small shallow bowl. 7. Pat dry the hard-boiled eggs with a paper towel. Roll each egg in the flour to coat. 8. Place one flour-coated egg on each sausage patty. Wrap the sausage patty around the egg so it completely encases the egg. 9. Coat the sausage-encased egg in the beaten egg, then in the bread crumbs. 10. Lightly spray the crisper plate with oil. Place the Scotch eggs in a single layer on the crisper plate and lightly spray them with oil. 11. Air-fry for 6 minutes. 12. Flip the Scotch eggs and lightly spray with oil. Air-fry for an additional 5 to 6 minutes, or until the sausage is fully cooked.

Per Serving: Calories 477; Fat 33.14g; Sodium 1431mg; Carbs 19.81g; Fibre 1.2g; Sugar 5.24g; Protein 23.66g

Cheesy Egg Stuffed Peppers

⏰ Prep: 15 minutes   🍲 Cook: 15 minutes   ⬚ Serves: 4

2 red peppers
Salt
Freshly ground black pepper
4 tablespoons crumbled cooked bacon
8 tablespoons shredded mozzarella cheese
4 large eggs
Extra-virgin olive oil, for the basket
4 teaspoons finely chopped fresh chives, for garnish (optional)

1. Install the crisper plate in the basket. 2. Select Air Fry mode, and set the cooking temperature at 180°C and adjust the cooking time to 15 minutes. Let the Ninja Air Fryer Max preheat. 3. Cut the peppers in half lengthwise from stem to base. Pop out the stem, then remove the seeds and membranes so each half looks like a shallow bowl. 4. Season the inside of each pepper half with salt and black pepper to taste. 5. Sprinkle 1 tablespoon chopped bacon into each pepper half, followed by 2 tablespoons mozzarella cheese. 6. Carefully crack one egg into each pepper half. 7. Lightly spray the crisper plate with oil. Place the pepper halves in a single layer on it. 8. Air-fry for 10 to 15 minutes. 9. Sprinkle each stuffed pepper with 1 teaspoon chives (optional) and serve.

Per Serving: Calories 182; Fat 13.76g; Sodium 677mg; Carbs 6.19g; Fibre 0.7g; Sugar 3.52g; Protein 9.14g

Nut and Berry Granola

🕐 **Prep: 15 minutes**　　🍲 **Cook: 12 minutes**　　📚 **Serves: 6**

120g rolled oats (not quick-cooking oats)
135g chopped pecans or walnuts, or a combination
3 tablespoons flaxseed
½ teaspoon cinnamon
⅛ teaspoon nutmeg
80g maple syrup
3 tablespoons vegetable oil
1 teaspoon vanilla
¼ teaspoon sea salt
60g dried blueberries
60g dried cherries

1. Select Bake mode, and set the cooking temperature at 180°C and adjust the cooking time to 12 minutes. 2. Let the Ninja Air Fryer Max preheat for 3 minutes. 3. In a large bowl, combine the oats, flaxseed, nuts, cinnamon, and nutmeg and mix well. 4. In a glass measuring cup, add the maple syrup, oil, vanilla, and salt and mix well. Add this mixture on top of the oat mixture and stir to combine. 5. Spread the mixture in a suitable round pan, and place the pan in the basket. 6. Bake the mixture for 12 minutes until the granola is golden brown and fragrant, stirring halfway through cooking time. 7. Transfer the granola to a serving bowl and let cool for 3 minutes. Stir in the dried blueberries and cherries. 8. Let stand until cool, then serve, or store in an airtight container at room temperature for up to 4 days.

Per Serving: Calories 296; Fat 19.44g; Sodium 103mg; Carbs 34.49g; Fibre 6.6g; Sugar 14.71g; Protein 7.35g

Glazed Ham Steak

🕐 **Prep: 5 minutes**　　🍲 **Cook: 15 minutes**　　📚 **Serves: 4**

2 tablespoons maple syrup
½ tablespoon apple cider vinegar
½ tablespoon Dijon mustard
¼ tablespoon brown sugar
1 (455g) ham steak, fully cooked

1. Install the crisper plate in the basket. 2. Select Air Fry mode, and set the cooking temperature at 190°C and adjust the cooking time to 15 minutes. Let the Ninja Air Fryer Max preheat. 3. In a small bowl, whisk together the maple syrup, vinegar, mustard, and brown sugar. 4. Remove the ham from the package and place it in the Ninja Air Fryer Max basket. Brush the marinade evenly over the top of the ham. 5. Air-fry the ham for 14 minutes, flipping the ham and brushing the ham with more marinade halfway through cooking time. When cooked, the ham should be lightly browned and the glaze should be caramelized.

Per Serving: Calories 144; Fat 3.93g; Sodium 1473mg; Carbs 8.33g; Fibre 0.1g; Sugar 6.45g; Protein 19.24g

| Chapter 1 Breakfast

Chapter 2 Vegetables and Sides

Air Fried Vegetable Skewers

⏱ **Prep: 40 minutes** 🍲 **Cook: 8 minutes** 📚 **Serves: 4**

1 medium courgette, trimmed and cut into 1cm slices
½ medium onion, peeled and cut into 2.5cm squares
1 medium red pepper, seeded and cut into 2.5cm squares
16 whole cremini mushrooms
70g basil pesto
½ teaspoon salt
¼ teaspoon ground black pepper

1. Divide courgette slices, onion, and pepper into eight even portions. Place on 15cm skewers for a total of eight kebabs. Add 2 mushrooms to each skewer and brush kebabs generously with pesto. 2. Sprinkle each kebab with salt and black pepper on all sides. 3. Select Air Fry mode, and set the cooking temperature at 190°C and adjust the cooking time to 8 minutes. Let the Ninja Air Fryer Max preheat for 3 minutes. 4. Once preheated, cook the kebabs for 8 minutes, turning them halfway through cooking. 5. Vegetables will be browned at the edges and tender-crisp when done. 6. Serve warm.
Per Serving: Calories 60; Fat 0.27g; Sodium 295mg; Carbs 14.34g; Fibre 2.6g; Sugar 2.3g; Protein 2.02g

Tasty Cheese Spinach Frittata

⏱ **Prep: 10 minutes** 🍲 **Cook: 20 minutes** 📚 **Serves: 4**

6 large eggs
120g heavy whipping cream
30g frozen chopped spinach, drained
100g shredded sharp Cheddar cheese
45g peeled and diced yellow onion
½ teaspoon salt
¼ teaspoon ground black pepper

1. Select Bake mode, and set the cooking temperature at 160°C and adjust the cooking time to 20 minutes. Let the Ninja Air Fryer Max preheat. 2. In a large bowl, whisk together the eggs and whipping cream. Whisk in spinach, Cheddar, onion, salt, and pepper. 3. Pour mixture into a suitable round nonstick baking dish. 4. Place the baking dish in the basket, and then cook the mixture for 20 minutes until firm and slightly browned. 5. Serve hot.
Per Serving: Calories 339; Fat 25g; Sodium 620mg; Carbs 4.3g; Fibre 0.9g; Sugar 2g; Protein 18g

Crispy Turnip Fries

⏰ **Prep: 5 minutes**   🍲 **Cook: 15 minutes**   ❖ **Serves: 4**

2 medium turnips, peeled and cut into ½cm fries
2 teaspoons avocado oil
2 teaspoons Everything Bagel seasoning, divided

1. In a medium bowl, toss fries with avocado oil and 1 teaspoon seasoning. 2. Install the crisper plate in the basket. 3. Select Air Fry mode, and set the cooking temperature at 200°C and adjust the cooking time to 15 minutes. Let the Ninja Air Fryer Max preheat. 4. When preheated, line the crisper plate with parchment paper, place the pieces on it. 5. Cook the food for 15 minutes, tossing them every 5 minutes. 6. Transfer the food to a medium serving plate, garnish with remaining seasoning, and serve warm.
Per Serving: Calories 46; Fat 4.3g; Sodium 230mg; Carbs 4.7g; Fibre 1.4g; Sugar 2g; Protein 1.35g

Tomato Avocado Boats

⏰ **Prep: 10 minutes**   🍲 **Cook: 5 minutes**   ❖ **Serves: 2**

150g seeded and diced tomatoes
1 tablespoon fresh lime juice
1 teaspoon lime zest
2 tablespoons chopped fresh coriander
1 small jalapeño, seeded and minced
2 cloves garlic, peeled and minced
1 tablespoon peeled and diced red onion
½ teaspoon salt
2 large avocados, halved and pitted
4 tablespoons vegan Cheddar shreds

1. Combine tomatoes, lime juice, lime zest, coriander, jalapeño, garlic, onion, and salt in a medium bowl. Cover the bowl and refrigerate until ready to use. 2. Install the crisper plate in the basket. 3. Select Air Fry mode, and set the cooking temperature at 180°C and adjust the cooking time to 4 minutes. Let the Ninja Air Fryer Max preheat. 4. When preheated, place the avocado halves on the crisper plate with cut-side up. Distribute cheese shreds to top of avocado halves. 5. Cook the food for 4 minutes. 6. Transfer avocados to a large serving plate, garnish with tomato mixture, and serve.
Per Serving: Calories 182; Fat 14.6g; Sodium 349mg; Carbs 12g; Fibre 5.9g; Sugar 2g; Protein 2g

Cauliflower Pizza Crust

⏰ **Prep: 20 minutes**   🍲 **Cook: 7 minutes**   📚 **Serves: 2**

1 (300g) steamer bag cauliflower, cooked according to package instructions
50g shredded sharp Cheddar cheese
1 large egg
2 tablespoons blanched finely ground almond flour
1 teaspoon Italian seasoning

1. Install the crisper plate in the basket. 2. Select Air Fry mode, and set the cooking temperature at 180°C and adjust the cooking time to 10 minutes. Let the Ninja Air Fryer Max preheat. 3. Let cooked cauliflower cool for 10 minutes. Using a kitchen towel, wring out excess moisture from cauliflower and place into a food processor. 4. Add Cheddar, egg, flour, and Italian seasoning to processor and pulse ten times until cauliflower is smooth and all ingredients are combined. 5. Line the crisper plate with two pieces of parchment paper; divide cauliflower mixture into two equal portions and press each on ungreased parchment. 6. Cook the food for 7 minutes, gently turning crusts halfway through cooking. 7. Store crusts in refrigerator in an airtight container up to 4 days or freeze between sheets of parchment in a sealable storage bag for up to 2 months.
Per Serving: Calories 237; Fat 14. 6g; Sodium 270mg; Carbs 10g; Fibre 5g; Sugar 4.5g; Protein 15. 4g

Cheese Soufflés with Mushrooms

⏰ **Prep: 15 minutes**   🍲 **Cook: 12 minutes**   📚 **Serves: 4**

3 large eggs, whites and yolks separated
50g sharp white Cheddar cheese
75g cream cheese, softened
¼ teaspoon cream of tartar
¼ teaspoon salt
¼ teaspoon ground black pepper
40g cremini mushrooms, sliced

1. Install the crisper plate in the basket. 2. Select Air Fry mode, and set the cooking temperature at 180°C and adjust the cooking time to 10 minutes. Let the Ninja Air Fryer Max preheat. 3. In a large bowl, whip the egg whites until stiff peaks form, about 2 minutes. 4. In a separate large bowl, beat Cheddar, egg yolks, cream cheese, cream of tartar, salt, and pepper together until combined. 5. Fold egg whites into cheese mixture, being careful not to stir. Fold in mushrooms, then pour mixture evenly into four ungreased 10 cm ramekins. 6. Place ramekins on the crisper plate. 7. Cook the food for 12 minutes. Eggs will be browned on the top and firm in the centre when done. 8. Serve warm.
Per Serving: Calories 190; Fat 14.64g; Sodium 367mg; Carbs 2.4g; Fibre 0g; Sugar 1.2g; Protein 10g

Courgette Fritters

⏱ **Prep: 45 minutes** 🍲 **Cook: 12 minutes** ❖ **Serves: 4**

1½ medium courgette, trimmed and grated
½ teaspoon salt, divided
1 large egg, whisked
¼ teaspoon garlic powder
25g grated Parmesan cheese

1. Place grated courgette on a kitchen towel and sprinkle with ¼ teaspoon salt. 2. Wrap in towel and let sit 30 minutes, then wring out as much excess moisture as possible. 3. Place courgette into a large bowl and mix with egg, remaining salt, garlic powder, and Parmesan. 4. Install the crisper plate in the basket. 5. Select Air Fry mode, and set the cooking temperature at 200°C and adjust the cooking time to 12 minutes. Let the Ninja Air Fryer Max preheat. 6. When preheated, cut a piece of parchment to fit the crisper plate. Divide mixture into four mounds, about ⅓ cup each, and press out into 10cm rounds on ungreased parchment. 7. Cook the fritters for 12 minutes, turning fritters halfway through cooking. Fritters will be crispy on the edges and tender but firm in the centre when done. 8. Serve warm.
Per Serving: Calories 76; Fat 1g; Sodium 426mg; Carbs 2.7g; Fibre 0.8g; Sugar 2g; Protein 4g

Homemade Roasted Brussels Sprouts with Bacon

⏱ **Prep: 10 minutes** 🍲 **Cook: 35 minutes** ❖ **Serves: 2**

600g Brussels sprouts
60ml fish sauce
60g bacon grease
6 strips bacon
Pepper to taste

1. Install the crisper plate in the basket. 2. Select Air Roast mode, and set the cooking temperature at 230°C and adjust the cooking time to 35 minutes. Let the Ninja Air Fryer Max preheat for 3 minutes. 3. De-stem and quarter the Brussels sprouts. 4. Mix them with the bacon grease and fish sauce. 4. Slice the bacon into small strips and cook. 5. Add the bacon and pepper to the sprouts. 6. Spread the food mixture onto a greased pan and place the pan on the crisper plate. 7. Roast the food for 35 minutes, stirring them every 5 minutes. 8. Serve warm.
Per Serving: Calories 452; Fat 31.86g; Sodium 3171mg; Carbs 34.86g; Fibre 13.7g; Sugar 9.96g; Protein 15.38g

Chapter 2 Vegetables and Sides

Prosciutto-Wrapped Asparagus

⏰ **Prep: 10 minutes**　🍳 **Cook: 12 minutes**　🍽 **Serves: 4**

75g prosciutto, sliced lengthwise into 18 slices
18 thick asparagus spears, trimmed of woody ends

1. Spiral wrap the prosciutto strips from the bottom of the asparagus to the top, stopping before covering the tip. 2. Install the crisper plate in the basket. 3. Select Air Fry mode, and set the cooking temperature at 200°C and adjust the cooking time to 12 minutes. Let the Ninja Air Fryer Max preheat. 4. When preheated, place the wrapped asparagus on the crisper plate. 5. Cook the food for 12 minutes until prosciutto is crisp, tossing the dish halfway through cooking. 6. Serve hot.
Per Serving: Calories 66; Fat 2.1g; Sodium 574mg; Carbs 3.5g; Fibre 0.98g; Sugar 1g; Protein 7.8g

Simple Courgette Ribbons

⏰ **Prep: 10 minutes**　🍳 **Cook: 5 minutes**　🍽 **Serves: 4**

2 medium courgettes (seed core discarded), peeled into thin ribbons
2 teaspoons butter, melted
¼ teaspoon salt
¼ teaspoon freshly ground black pepper

1. In a medium bowl, toss courgette ribbons with butter, salt, and pepper. 2. Install the crisper plate in the basket. 3. Select Air Fry mode, and set the cooking temperature at 135°C and adjust the cooking time to 3 minutes. Let the Ninja Air Fryer Max preheat. 4. When preheated, place the courgette ribbons on the crisper plate. 5. Cook the food for 3 minutes, tossing them halfway through. 6. Serve warm.
Per Serving: Calories 38; Fat 1.6g; Sodium 150mg; Carbs 3.7g; Fibre 0.9g; Sugar 2g; Protein 1g

Garlic Broccoli with Sriracha

⏰ **Prep: 15 minutes**　🍲 **Cook: 15 minutes**　Servings: 4

455g broccoli, cut into florets
1 teaspoon rice vinegar
2 teaspoons sriracha
2 tablespoons soy sauce
1 tablespoon garlic, minced
5 drops liquid stevia
1½ tablespoons sesame oil
Salt

1. In a suitable bowl, toss together broccoli, garlic, oil, and salt. 2. Install the crisper plate in the air fryer basket and spread broccoli in the basket. Select Air Fry mode, set the cooking temperature to 200°C, and adjust the cooking time to 15 minutes. Press the START/STOP to begin cooking. 3. Meanwhile, mix the soy sauce, vinegar, liquid stevia, and sriracha in a microwave-safe bowl and microwave for almost 10 seconds. 4. Transfer broccoli to a bowl and toss well with soy mixture to coat. 5. Sprinkle with sesame seeds if desired. Serve and enjoy.

Healthy Tamari Green Beans

⏰ **Prep: 15 minutes**　🍲 **Cook: 10 minutes**　Servings: 2

225g green beans, trimmed
1 teaspoon sesame oil
1 tablespoon tamari

1. Add all the recipe ingredients into a suitable mixing bowl and toss well. 2. Install the crisper plate in the air fryer basket and grease with cooking spray. Transfer the green beans to the air fryer basket. Select Air Fry mode, set the cooking temperature at 200°C, and adjust the cooking time to 10 minutes. Press the START/STOP to begin cooking. Toss halfway through. 3. Sprinkle with sesame seeds if desired. Serve and enjoy.

Roasted Brussels Sprouts

⏰ **Prep: 15 minutes**   🍲 **Cook: 8 minutes**   Servings: 4

455g Brussels sprouts, cleaned and trimmed
1 teaspoon garlic powder
1 teaspoon dried parsley
2 teaspoons olive oil
½ teaspoon dried thyme
¼ teaspoon salt

1. Add all the recipe ingredients into a suitable bowl and toss well. 2. Install the crisper plate in the air fryer basket and pour the Brussels sprout mixture into the air fryer basket. Select Air Fry mode, set the cooking temperature to 200°C, and adjust the cooking time to 8 minutes. Press the START/STOP to begin cooking. 3. Serve and enjoy.

Garlic Roasted Cherry Tomatoes

⏰ **Prep: 15 minutes**   🍲 **Cook: 15 minutes**   Servings: 4

1 tablespoon olive oil
455g cherry tomatoes, halved
1 tablespoon dill, chopped
6 garlic cloves, minced
1 tablespoon balsamic vinegar
Black pepper and salt to the taste

1. In a pan that fits the air fryer, combine all the recipe ingredients and toss gently. 2. Install the crisper plate in the air fryer basket and put the pan in the air fryer basket. Select Air Fry mode, set the cooking temperature to 195°C, and adjust the cooking time to 15 minutes. Press the START/STOP to begin cooking. 3. Divide between plates and serve.

Chapter 2 Vegetables and Sides | 29

Chapter 3 Snacks and Starters

Bacon-Wrapped Sausage

⏱ **Prep: 5 minutes**　　🍲 **Cook: 5 minutes**　　📚 **Serves: 2**

5 Italian chicken sausages
10 slices bacon

1. Install the crisper plate in the basket. 2. Select Air Fry mode, and set the cooking temperature at 190°C and adjust the cooking time to 5 minutes. Let the Ninja Air Fryer Max preheat for 3 minutes. 3. Cut the sausage into four pieces, and slice the bacon in half. 4. Wrap the bacon over the sausage and then skewer them. 5. Air-fry the food for 5 minutes or until browned.
Per Serving: Calories 621; Fat 58.81g; Sodium 963mg; Carbs 2.12g; Fibre 0g; Sugar 1.08g; Protein 20.49g

Fluffy Cloud Eggs

⏱ **Prep: 5 minutes**　　🍲 **Cook: 10 minutes**　　📚 **Serves: 2**

2 large eggs, whites and yolks separated
¼ teaspoon salt
¼ teaspoon dried oregano
2 tablespoons chopped fresh chives
2 teaspoons salted butter, melted

1. In a large bowl, whip the egg whites until stiff peaks form, about 3 minutes. 2. Place egg whites evenly into two ungreased 10cm ramekins. 3. Sprinkle evenly with salt, oregano, and chives. Place 1 whole egg yolk in centre of each ramekin and drizzle with butter. 4. Install the crisper plate in the basket. 5. Select Air Fry mode, and set the cooking temperature at 180°C and adjust the cooking time to 8 minutes. Let the Ninja Air Fryer Max preheat. 6. When preheated, place ramekins on the crisper plate. 7. Cook for 8 minutes. 8. Egg whites will be fluffy and browned when done. 9. Serve warm.
Per Serving: Calories 120; Fat 8.96g; Sodium 390mg; Carbs 0.9g; Fibre 0g; Sugar 0g; Protein 6.08g

Broccoli Cheddar Casserole

⏰ **Prep:** 15 minutes　🍳 **Cook:** 35 minutes　🍽 **Serves:** 6

360g broccoli florets
60ml ranch dressing
50g sharp cheddar cheese, shredded
60g heavy whipping cream
Salt and pepper to taste

1. Select Bake mode, and set the cooking temperature at 190°C and adjust the cooking time to 35 minutes. Let the Ninja Air Fryer Max preheat for 3 minutes. 2. Combine all ingredients in a bowl until the broccoli is well-covered. 3. Transfer the broccoli florets to a suitable casserole dish, and place the dish in the basket. 4. Bake the food for 35 minutes until tender, stirring them after 30 minutes of cooking time. 5. Serve warm.

Per Serving: Calories 111; Fat 10.17g; Sodium 172mg; Carbs 1.86g; Fibre 0.8g; Sugar 0.74g; Protein 3.76g

Crispy Flax Cheddar Cheese Chips

⏰ **Prep:** 10 minutes　🍳 **Cook:** 15 minutes　🍽 **Serves:** 2

150g cheddar cheese
4 tablespoons ground flaxseed meal
Seasonings of your choice

1. Install the crisper plate in the basket. 2. Select Bake mode, and set the cooking temperature at 220°C and adjust the cooking time to 15 minutes. Let the Ninja Air Fryer Max preheat for 3 minutes. 3. Spoon 2 tablespoons of cheddar cheese into a mound, onto a non-stick pad. 4. Spread out a pinch of flax seed on each chip and season them with the seasonings you like. 5. Bake the food for 10 to 15 minutes. 6. Serve warm.

Per Serving: Calories 512; Fat 42.17g; Sodium 644mg; Carbs 7.27g; Fibre 5.6g; Sugar 0.6g; Protein 27.57g

Crispy Mozzarella Cheese Sticks

⏰ **Prep: 50 minutes**   🍲 **Cook: 10 minutes**   ⬧ **Serves: 4**

6 x 25g mozzarella string cheese sticks
1 teaspoons dried parsley
50g panko bread crumbs
2 eggs

1. Install the crisper plate in the basket. 2. Select Bake mode, and set the cooking temperature at 200°C and adjust the cooking time to 45 minutes. Let the Ninja Air Fryer Max preheat for 3 minutes. 3. Halve the mozzarella sticks and freeze for 45 minutes. 4. Combine the dried parsley, and bread crumbs in a bowl. 5. Beat the eggs in a separate bowl. 6. Dip the sticks into the eggs, then into the bread crumbs one by one, making sure to coat them all over. 7. When preheated, line the crisper plate with parchment paper, and arrange the sticks on it, and then cook them for 10 minutes until the sticks are golden brown. 8. Serve warm.
Per Serving: Calories 187; Fat 8.93g; Sodium 595mg; Carbs 3.76g; Fibre 0.8g; Sugar 0.97g; Protein 22.42g

Garlicky Radish Chips

⏰ **Prep: 10 minutes**   🍲 **Cook: 5 minutes**   ⬧ **Serves: 1**

480ml water
455g radishes
½ teaspoons garlic powder
¼ teaspoons onion powder
2 tablespoons coconut oil, melted

1. Boil the water. 2. Slice off the tops and bottoms of the radishes and shave them into thin slices of equal size. 3. Put the radish chips in the pot of boiling water and let cook for 5 minutes until they are translucent. Dry them with the paper towel. 4. Add the radish chips, garlic powder, onion powder, and melted coconut oil into a bowl and toss to coat. 5. Install the crisper plate in the basket. Select Air Fry mode, and set the cooking temperature at 160°C and adjust the cooking time to 5 minutes. 6. Let the Ninja Air Fryer Max preheat. When preheated, place the chips on the crisper plate. 7. Cook the chips for 5 minutes until crispy. 8. Serve immediately.
Per Serving: Calories 323; Fat 27.67g; Sodium 106mg; Carbs 20.24g; Fibre 7.5g; Sugar 11.42g; Protein 3.05g

Chapter 3 Snacks and Starters

Buffalo Cauliflower Florets

⏱ **Prep: 10 minutes**   🍲 **Cook: 5 minutes**   📚 **Serves: 2**

½ packet dry ranch seasoning
2 tablespoons salted butter, melted
1 head cauliflower, cut into florets
60ml buffalo sauce

1. Install the crisper plate in the basket. 2. Select Air Fry mode, and set the cooking temperature at 200°C and adjust the cooking time to 45 minutes. Let the Ninja Air Fryer Max preheat for 3 minutes. 3. In a bowl, combine the dry ranch seasoning and butter. Toss with the cauliflower florets to coat and transfer them to the basket. 4. Cook the food for 5 minutes, tossing them halfway through. 5. Pour the buffalo sauce over the dish and enjoy.

Per Serving: Calories 344; Fat 9.03g; Sodium 3019mg; Carbs 55.29g; Fibre 13.3g; Sugar 23.61g; Protein 9.98g

Roasted Taco Cauliflower

⏱ **Prep: 5 minutes**   🍲 **Cook: 7 minutes**   📚 **Serves: 2**

180g cauliflower florets, chopped
2 tablespoons coconut oil, melted
2½ teaspoons taco seasoning mix
1 medium lime
2 tablespoons coriander, chopped

1. Install the crisper plate in the basket. 2. Select Air Roast mode, and set the cooking temperature at 180°C and adjust the cooking time to 7 minutes. Let the Ninja Air Fryer Max preheat for 3 minutes. 3. Mix the cauliflower with the melted coconut oil and the taco seasoning, ensuring to coat the florets all over. 4. Cook the food for 5 minutes, tossing them a few times during the cooking. 5. Squeeze the lime juice over the cauliflower and season with the coriander. Toss and enjoy.

Per Serving: Calories 161; Fat 13.92g; Sodium 289mg; Carbs 9.27g; Fibre 2.7g; Sugar 2.81g; Protein 2.33g

Cheesy Cauliflower Bites

⏰ **Prep: 5 minutes**   🍲 **Cook: 16 minutes**   🍽 **Serves: 3**

180g cauliflower florets
75g cheddar cheese, shredded
90g onion, chopped
1 teaspoon seasoning salt
2 tablespoons butter, melted
2 cloves garlic, minced

1. Install the crisper plate in the basket. 2. Select Air Fry mode, and set the cooking temperature at 200°C and adjust the cooking time to 16 minutes. Let the Ninja Air Fryer Max preheat for 3 minutes. 3. Pulse the cauliflower florets in the food processor until they become crumbly. Remove all the moisture from the cauliflower. 4. Combine the cauliflower with the cheese, onion, seasoning salt, and melted butter in a bowl. Roll the mixture into balls. 5. Air-fry the balls for 14 to 16 minutes. 6. Serve hot.
Per Serving: Calories 230; Fat 19.07g; Sodium 1071mg; Carbs 6.44g; Fibre 1.8g; Sugar 2.29g; Protein 9.72g

Rosemary Potato Chips with Sour Cream

⏰ **Prep: 10 minutes**   🍲 **Cook: 35 minutes**   🍽 **Serves: 4**

2 large potatoes, peel and sliced
1 tablespoons rosemary
85g sour cream
¼ teaspoons salt

1. Install the crisper plate in the basket. 2. Select Air Fry mode, and set the cooking temperature at 160°C and adjust the cooking time to 35 minutes. Let the Ninja Air Fryer Max preheat for 3 minutes. 3. Place the potato slices in water and allow to absorb for 30 minutes. 4. Drain the potato slices and place the coated potato slices in the basket and cook for 35 minutes. 6. Transfer to a large bowl and toss with rosemary. Serve hot with the sour cream.
Per Serving: Calories 176; Fat 2.82g; Sodium 177mg; Carbs 34.08g; Fibre 4.1g; Sugar 1.49g; Protein 4.61g

Chapter 3 Snacks and Starters

Balsamic Roasted Brussels Sprouts

⏰ **Prep: 5 minutes** 🍲 **Cook: 10 minutes** 📚 **Serves: 2**

180g Brussels sprouts, sliced in half
1 tablespoon balsamic vinegar
1 tablespoon olive oil
¼ teaspoons salt

1. Install the crisper plate in the basket. 2. Select Air Fry mode, and set the cooking temperature at 200°C and adjust the cooking time to 10 minutes. Let the Ninja Air Fryer Max preheat for 3 minutes. 3. Toss all of the ingredients together in a bowl, coating the Brussels sprouts well. 4. Place the sprouts in the basket and air-fry for 10 minutes, tossing them at the halfway point. 5. Serve hot.
Per Serving: Calories 105; Fat 7.01g; Sodium 315mg; Carbs 9.24g; Fibre 3.3g; Sugar 3.13g; Protein 3.01g

Cheese Drop Biscuits

⏰ **Prep: 15 minutes** 🍲 **Cook: 20 minutes** 📚 **Serves: 8**

90g plain flour
½ teaspoon salt
¼ teaspoon cayenne pepper
¼ teaspoon smoked paprika
¼ teaspoon black pepper
Dash garlic powder (optional)
55g butter, softened
100g shredded sharp cheddar cheese, at room temperature
Olive oil spray

1. In a small bowl, combine the flour, cayenne, salt, paprika, pepper, and garlic powder, if using. 2. Cream the butter and cheese until smooth. Gently add the seasoned flour and process until the dough is well combined, smooth, and no longer sticky. 3. Divide the dough into 32 equal-size pieces. On a lightly floured surface, roll each piece into a small ball. 4. Install the crisper plate in the basket. 5. Select Air Fry mode, and set the cooking temperature at 180°C and adjust the cooking time to 5 minutes. Let the Ninja Air Fryer Max preheat. 6. When preheated, spray the crisper plate with oil spray, and place 16 cheese drops on the crisper plate. 7. Cook the food for 10 minutes. Cook them in batches. 8. Cool the cheese drops completely on the wire rack. Store in an airtight container until ready to serve, or up to 1 or 2 days.
Per Serving: Calories 161; Fat 11.48g; Sodium 298mg; Carbs 9.3g; Fibre 0.4g; Sugar 0.1g; Protein 5.27g

Crunchy Spanish Peanuts

⏰ Prep: 15 minutes   🍲 Cook: 15 minutes   🍽 Serves: 4

5 tablespoons chickpea flour
½ teaspoon cumin seeds
¼ teaspoon ground turmeric
¼ teaspoon salt, plus more for seasoning if desired
¼ to ½ teaspoon cayenne pepper
2 tablespoons vegetable oil
3 tablespoons water
145g red Spanish peanuts or unsalted roasted peanuts
Vegetable oil spray
Prepared chaat masala or amchoor (dried mango powder), optional

1. In a medium bowl, add the chickpea flour, cumin seeds, turmeric, salt, and cayenne. Add the oil and stir to combine. Add the water and stir to make a thick, pancake-like batter. Add the peanuts and stir until well blended. 2. Install the crisper plate in the basket. 3. Select Air Fry mode, and set the cooking temperature at 160°C and adjust the cooking time to 10 minutes. Let the Ninja Air Fryer Max preheat. 4. When preheated, line the crisper plate with parchment paper, and pour the peanut mixture on it. 5. Cook the mixture for 10 minutes. 6. Open the Ninja Air Fryer Max and break up the peanuts and batter. Remove the parchment paper and let the peanuts sit directly on the bottom of the Ninja Air Fryer Max basket. Spray the peanuts generously with the vegetable oil spray. 7. Air-fry them at 200°C for 5 minutes or until the outsides of the peanuts are crisp. 8. Transfer the peanuts to a rimmed baking sheet and shake well. Sprinkle them with chaat masala or amchoor, if using. Let peanuts cool for 10 minutes before serving. 9. Store in an airtight container.

Per Serving: Calories 302; Fat 25.37g; Sodium 155mg; Carbs 10.83g; Fibre 4.1g; Sugar 0.79g; Protein 11.98g

Pigs in a Blanket

⏰ Prep: 15 minutes   🍲 Cook: 8 minutes   🍽 Serves: 8

1 sheet frozen puff pastry
Plain flour
60g coarse-ground Dijon mustard
32 fully cooked cocktail sausages
1 large egg, beaten
2 tablespoons sesame seeds

1. Thaw the puff pastry according to package instructions. 2. Lightly flour a work surface. Roll the pastry to a 45 × 30cm rectangle. Spread the mustard over the pastry. Cut the large rectangle lengthwise in half, then cut each smaller rectangle into 16 equal pieces for a total of 32 rectangles, about 5 × 8cm each. 3. Place one sausage on a short end of a pastry rectangle and roll up. Moisten the edge of the pastry with a little water if necessary to seal. Use a fork to prick the pastry in one or two places. 4. Repeat to make 32 pigs in blankets. Brush each pastry with beaten egg and sprinkle with sesame seeds. 5. Install the crisper plate in the basket. 6. Select Air Fry mode, and set the cooking temperature at 180°C and adjust the cooking time to 8 minutes. Let the Ninja Air Fryer Max preheat. 7. When preheated, place the wrapped sausages on the crisper plate. 8. Cook the sausages for 8 minutes until the pastry is golden brown. You can cook them in batches. 9. Serve hot.

Per Serving: Calories 323; Fat 20.87g; Sodium 950mg; Carbs 25.58g; Fibre 3.5g; Sugar 0.92g; Protein 9.42g

Shakshuka Harissa

🕐 Prep: 15 minutes 🍲 Cook: 15 minutes 🍽 Serves: 4

For the Harissa:
120ml olive oil
6 cloves garlic, minced
2 tablespoons smoked paprika
1 tablespoon ground coriander
1 tablespoon ground cumin
1 teaspoon ground caraway
1 teaspoon salt
½ to 1 teaspoon cayenne pepper

For the Shakshuka:
150g canned diced tomatoes with their liquid
4 large eggs
Chopped fresh parsley (optional)
Black pepper (optional)

1. In a medium microwave-safe bowl, combine all the ingredients. Microwave on high for 1 minute, stirring halfway through the cooking time. 2. In a suitable heatproof pan, combine the tomatoes with 1 teaspoon of the harissa and stir until well combined. Taste and add more harissa if you want the sauce to be spicier. 3. Carefully crack the eggs into the tomato mixture, taking care to not break the yolks. Cover the pan with foil. 4. Install the crisper plate in the basket. 5. Select Air Fry mode, and set the cooking temperature at 180°C and adjust the cooking time to 5 minutes. Let the Ninja Air Fryer Max preheat. 6. When preheated, place the pan on the crisper plate. 7. Cook the food for 15 minutes. Remove the foil. For a runny yolk, cook for an additional 3 minutes; for a more set yolk, cook an additional 5 minutes. 8. Garnish with fresh parsley and black pepper, if desired.

Per Serving: Calories 376; Fat 32.48g; Sodium 602mg; Carbs 19.66g; Fibre 3.8g; Sugar 13.14g; Protein 4.69g

Tasty Masala Omelet

🕐 Prep: 10 minutes 🍲 Cook: 15 minutes 🍽 Serves: 2

4 large eggs
90g diced onion
75g diced tomato
10g chopped fresh coriander
1 jalapeño, seeded and finely chopped
½ teaspoon ground turmeric
½ teaspoon salt
½ teaspoon cayenne pepper
Olive oil for greasing the pan

1. In a large bowl, beat the eggs. Stir in the onion, tomato, coriander, jalapeño, turmeric, salt, and cayenne. 2. Generously grease a suitable baking pan. 3. Pour the egg mixture into the prepared pan. 4. Install the crisper plate in the basket. 5. Select Air Fry mode, and set the cooking temperature at 120°C and adjust the cooking time to 12 minutes. Let the Ninja Air Fryer Max preheat. 6. When preheated, place the pan on the crisper plate. 7. Cook the food for 12 minutes. 8. Carefully unmold and cut the omelet into four pieces.

Per Serving: Calories 141; Fat 9.28g; Sodium 604mg; Carbs 8.32g; Fibre 1.6g; Sugar 3.62g; Protein 6.66g

Chapter 4 Poultry

Cajun Chicken Breasts

⏱ **Prep: 15 minutes**   🍲 **Cook: 12 minutes**   ≋ **Serves: 2**

2 medium-sized chicken breasts, skinless and boneless
1 tablespoon olive oil
3 tablespoons Cajun seasoning
½ teaspoon salt

1. Rub the chicken breasts with Cajun seasoning, salt, and sprinkle with olive oil. 2. Air-fry the food in the Ninja Air Fryer Max at 190°C for 7 minutes. Turn over and cook for an additional 4 minutes. 3. Slice and serve.
Per Serving: Calories 600; Fat 33.58g; Sodium 1690mg; Carbs 7.45g; Fibre 1.7g; Sugar 1.39g; Protein 61.04g

Marinated Chicken Drumsticks

⏱ **Prep: 15 minutes**   🍲 **Cook: 20 minutes**   ≋ **Serves: 4**

1 clove garlic, crushed
Salt and black pepper to taste
4 chicken drumsticks
1 tablespoon olive oil
1 teaspoon chili powder
½ tablespoon mustard
1 teaspoon liquid Stevia

1. Mix garlic with liquid Stevia, mustard, salt, black pepper, chili powder and oil. 2. Rub drumsticks with marinade and marinate for 20 minutes. 3. Place drumsticks on the crisper plate in the basket. Air-fry the food in the Ninja Air Fryer Max at 200°C for 10 minutes. 4. Lower the temperature to 150°C and cook for an additional 10 minutes. 5. Serve warm.
Per Serving: Calories 248; Fat 15.56g; Sodium 180mg; Carbs 1.94g; Fibre 0.5g; Sugar 0.65g; Protein 23.96g

Spicy Chicken Wings

⏱ **Prep: 15 minutes**　　🍳 **Cook: 30 minutes**　　🍽 **Serves: 6**

1 teaspoon liquid Stevia
1 tablespoon Worcestershire sauce
115g butter, melted
1.8 kg chicken wings
120ml hot sauce
½ teaspoon salt

1. Add Stevia, Worcestershire sauce, butter, salt, and hot sauce in a bowl and mix well. Set aside. 2. Place chicken wings on the crisper plate in the basket. Air-fry the food in the Ninja Air Fryer Max at 190°C for 25 minutes. 3. Shake basket halfway through. 4. After 25 minutes, change the temperature to 200°C and cook the meat for 5 minutes. 5. Add air-fried chicken wings into the bowl with mixture and toss well. Enjoy.
Per Serving: Calories 521; Fat 26.15g; Sodium 1096mg; Carbs 0.92g; Fibre 0.1g; Sugar 0.54g; Protein 66.71g

Cheesy Chicken and Courgette Casserole

⏱ **Prep: 30 minutes**　　🍳 **Cook: 60 minutes**　　🍽 **Serves: 8**

900g chicken mince
2 (125g) cans tomato sauce
⅛ teaspoon Stevia
Salt and pepper to taste
400g ricotta cheese
2 courgettes, sliced or cubed
3 eggs
2 tablespoons soy sauce
½ small onion, diced

1. In a bowl, add chicken, onion, soy sauce, and 2 eggs. 2. Add chicken mince mixture to baking dish. Add courgette on top. 3. In a bowl, mix egg, ricotta cheese, salt, and pepper. 4. Add the cheese mixture on top of courgettes. In another bowl, mix stevia and tomato sauce. 5. Add on top of cheese and bake them at 190°C for 1 hour.
Per Serving: Calories 333; Fat 22.18g; Sodium 311mg; Carbs 6.42g; Fibre 2.4g; Sugar 4.36g; Protein 26.26g

Flavourful Buffalo Chicken Wings

⏲ **Prep: 15 minutes**   🍲 **Cook: 25 minutes**   🍽 **Serves: 3**

900g chicken wings
240ml buffalo sauce
Salt and black pepper to taste

1. Wash and dry the chicken wings. 2. Place the chicken wings into a bowl and season with salt and pepper. 3. Place the chicken wings on the crisper plate in the basket and air-fry the wings in the Ninja Air Fryer Max at 190°C for 15 minutes. 4. Put wings into a bowl of buffalo sauce and mix well. Return them to Ninja Air Fryer Max and cook for an additional 6 minutes. 5. Serve warm with sauce you like if desired.

Per Serving: Calories 412; Fat 10.88g; Sodium 857mg; Carbs 7.24g; Fibre 1.8g; Sugar 4.18g; Protein 68.07g

Easy Marinated Chicken Wings

⏲ **Prep: 15 minutes**   🍲 **Cook: 12 minutes**   🍽 **Serves: 2**

16 chicken wings
2 tablespoons lime juice
2 tablespoons honey
2 tablespoons soy sauce
Salt and pepper to taste

1. Mix all ingredients in a mixing bowl. Marinate the mix for 6 hours in the fridge. 2. Place the chicken wings on the crisper plate in the basket. Air-fry the food in the Ninja Air Fryer Max at 180°C for 12 minutes. 3. Flip chicken wings over halfway through. 4. Serve with a wedge of lemon.

Per Serving: Calories 415; Fat 11.15g; Sodium431mg; Carbs 24.67g; Fibre 0.8g; Sugar 21.72g; Protein 52.68g

Almond-Crusted Chicken Nuggets

⏰ Prep: 10 minutes　🍲 Cook: 13 minutes　🍽 Serves: 4

1 egg white
1 tablespoon freshly squeezed lemon juice
½ teaspoon dried basil
½ teaspoon ground paprika
455g low-sodium boneless skinless chicken breasts, cut into 3.5cm cubes
50g ground almonds
2 slices low-sodium whole-wheat bread, crumbled

1. In a shallow bowl, beat the egg white, lemon juice, basil, and paprika with a fork until foamy. 2. Add the chicken and stir to coat. 3. On a plate, mix the almonds and bread crumbs. 4. Toss the chicken cubes in the almond and bread crumb mixture until coated. 5. Bake the nuggets in the Ninja Air Fryer Max at 200°C for 10 to 13 minutes, or until the chicken reaches an internal temperature of 75°C on a meat thermometer. 6. Serve immediately.

Per Serving: Calories 246; Fat 8.12g; Sodium 138mg; Carbs 13g; Fibre 3.4g; Sugar 3g; Protein 32.1g

Delicious Chicken Breasts

⏰ Prep: 10 minutes　🍲 Cook: 20 minutes　🍽 Serves: 4

80g no-salt-added tomato sauce
2 tablespoons low-sodium grainy mustard
2 tablespoons apple cider vinegar
1 tablespoon honey
2 garlic cloves, minced
1 jalapeño pepper, minced
3 tablespoons minced onion
4 (125g) low-sodium boneless skinless chicken breasts

1. In a small bowl, stir together the tomato sauce, mustard, cider vinegar, honey, garlic, jalapeño, and onion. 2. Brush the chicken breasts with some sauce and air-roast them in the Ninja Air Fryer Max at 190°C for 10 minutes. 3. Remove the Ninja Air Fryer Max basket and turn the chicken; brush with more sauce, and air-roast them for 5 minutes more. 4. Remove the Ninja Air Fryer Max basket and turn the chicken again; brush with more sauce. Cook them for 3 to 5 minutes more, or until the chicken reaches an internal temperature of 75°C on a meat thermometer. Discard any remaining sauce. 5. Serve immediately.

Per Serving: Calories 192; Fat 2.2g; Sodium 92mg; Carbs 7.2g; Fibre 1.23g; Sugar 7g; Protein 30g

Buttermilk Fried Chicken Breasts

⏱ **Prep: 10 minutes**   🍲 **Cook: 25 minutes**   ❖ **Serves: 4**

4 (125g) low-sodium boneless skinless chicken breasts, pounded to about 1cm thick
120ml buttermilk
65g plain flour
2 tablespoons cornflour
1 teaspoon dried thyme
1 teaspoon ground paprika
1 egg white
1 tablespoon olive oil

1. In a shallow bowl, mix the chicken and buttermilk. Let stand for 10 minutes. 2. In another shallow bowl, mix the flour, cornflour, thyme, and paprika. 3. In a small bowl, whisk the egg white and olive oil. Quickly stir this egg mixture into the flour mixture so the dry ingredients are evenly moistened. 4. Remove the chicken from the buttermilk and shake off any excess liquid. Dip each piece of chicken into the flour mixture to coat. 5. Air-fry the chicken in the Ninja Air Fryer Max basket at 200°C for 17 to 23 minutes until the chicken reaches an internal temperature of 75°C on a meat thermometer. 6. Serve immediately.

Per Serving: Calories 226; Fat 6.12g; Sodium 110mg; Carbs 7g; Fibre 0.g; Sugar 1g; Protein 35g

Crispy Chicken Nuggets

⏱ **Prep: 10 minutes**   🍲 **Cook: 10 minutes**   ❖ **Serves: 4**

455g boneless, skinless chicken breasts
Chicken seasoning or rub
Salt
Pepper
2 eggs
6 tablespoons bread crumbs
2 tablespoons panko bread crumbs
Cooking oil

1. Cut the chicken breasts into 2.5cm pieces. 2. In a large bowl, mix the chicken pieces with chicken seasoning, salt, and pepper to taste. 3. In a small bowl, beat the eggs. In another bowl, combine the bread crumbs and panko. 4. Dip the chicken pieces in the eggs and then the bread crumbs. 5. Place the nuggets on the crisper plate in the basket. 6. Air-fry the food in the Ninja Air Fryer Max at 200°C for 8 minutes, stirring them halfway through. You can cook them in batches.

Per Serving: Calories 460; Fat 17.74g; Sodium 672mg; Carbs 37.56g; Fibre 2.3g; Sugar 4.6g; Protein 34.65g

| Chapter 4 Poultry

Buttermilk Fried Chicken Wings

⏱ **Prep: 10 minutes**   🍲 **Cook: 20 minutes**   📚 **Serves: 4**

16 chicken drumettes (party wings)
1 teaspoon garlic powder
Chicken seasoning or rub
Pepper
65g plain flour
60ml low-fat buttermilk
Cooking oil

1. Place the chicken in a sealable plastic bag. Add the garlic powder, then add chicken seasoning or rub and pepper to taste. Seal the bag. Shake the bag thoroughly to combine the seasonings and coat the chicken. 2. Pour the flour into a second sealable plastic bag. 3. Pour the buttermilk into a bowl large enough to dunk the chicken. One at a time, dunk the drumettes in the buttermilk, then place them in the bag of flour. Seal and shake to thoroughly coat the chicken. 4. Spray the Ninja Air Fryer Max basket with cooking oil. 5. Transfer the chicken from the bag to the crisper plate in the basket. Spray the chicken with cooking oil, being sure to cover the bottom layer. 6. Air-fry the food in the Ninja Air Fryer Max at 200°C for 5 minutes. 7. Remove the basket and shake it to ensure all of the chicken pieces will cook fully. 8. Return the basket to the Ninja Air Fryer Max and continue to cook the chicken. Repeat shaking every 5 minutes until 20 minutes has passed.
Per Serving: Calories 233; Fat 6.07g; Sodium 159mg; Carbs 12.91g; Fibre 0.6g; Sugar 0.11g; Protein 29.61g

Air Fryer Crispy Whole Chicken Wings

⏱ **Prep: 10 minutes**   🍲 **Cook: 20 minutes**   📚 **Serves: 4**

8 whole chicken wings
Juice of ½ lemon
½ teaspoon garlic powder
1 teaspoon onion powder
Salt
Pepper
60ml low-fat buttermilk
65g plain flour
Cooking oil

1. Place the wings in a sealable plastic bag. Drizzle the wings with the lemon juice. Season the wings with the garlic powder, onion powder, and salt and pepper to taste. 2. Seal the bag, shake thoroughly to combine the seasonings, and coat the wings. 3. Place the buttermilk and the flour into separate bowls large enough to dip the wings. 4. Spray the Ninja Air Fryer Max basket with cooking oil. 5. One at a time, dip the chicken wings in the buttermilk and then the flour. 6. Place the chicken wings on the crisper plate in the basket. Spray the wings with cooking oil, being sure to spray the bottom layer. 7. Air-fry the food in the Ninja Air Fryer Max at 200°C for 5 minutes. 8. Remove the basket and shake to ensure all of the pieces will cook fully. 9. Return the basket to the Ninja Air Fryer Max and continue to cook the chicken. 10. Repeat shaking every 5 minutes until a total of 20 minutes has passed.
Per Serving: Calories 161; Fat 4.01g; Sodium 151mg; Carbs 13.18g; Fibre 0.6g; Sugar 0.29g; Protein 16.84g

Crispy Popcorn Chicken

⏰ Prep: 15 minutes   🍲 Cook: 12 minutes   Servings: 6

4 eggs
680g chicken breasts, diced into small chunks
1 teaspoon paprika
½ teaspoon garlic powder
1 teaspoon onion powder
40g pork rind, crushed
30g coconut flour
Black pepper
Salt

1. In a suitable bowl, mix together coconut flour, black pepper, and salt. 2. In another bowl, whisk eggs until combined. 3. Take 1 more bowl and mix together pork panko, paprika, garlic powder, and onion powder. 4. Add chicken pieces in a suitable mixing bowl. Sprinkle coconut flour mixture over chicken and toss well. 5. Dip chicken pieces in the prepared egg mixture, coat with pork panko mixture, and place on a plate. 6. Place the crisper plate in the air fryer basket and grease it with cooking spray. Transfer the prepared chicken to the air fryer basket. Select Air Fry mode, and set the cooking temperature at 200°C, and adjust the cooking time to 12 minutes. Press the START/STOP to begin cooking. Shake the basket halfway through. 7. Serve and enjoy.

Lemon Roasted Whole Chicken

⏰ Prep: 15 minutes   🍲 Cook: 28 minutes   Servings: 2

455g whole chicken
1 lemon, juiced
1 teaspoon lemon zest
1 tablespoon soy sauce
1½ tablespoon honey

1. Place all of the recipe ingredients in a suitable bowl and combine well. Refrigerate for 1 hour. 2. Install the crisper plate in the air fryer basket. Put the marinated and seasoned chicken in the air fryer basket. 3. Air fry at 160°C for 18 minutes. 4. Increase the temperature to 175°C and cook for another 10 minutes or until the chicken has turned light brown. 5. Serve.

Turkey Breasts with Shallot

⏰ **Prep: 15 minutes**   🍲 **Cook: 31 minutes**   Servings: 4

1 big turkey breast, skinless, boneless, and cubed
1 tablespoon olive oil
¼ teaspoon sweet paprika
Black pepper and salt to the taste
235 ml chicken stock
3 tablespoons. butter, melted
4 shallots, chopped

1. Heat a pan that fits the air fryer with the olive oil and the butter over medium-high heat, add the turkey cubes, and brown for 3 minutes on each side. 2. Add the shallots, stir, and sauté for 5 minutes more. 3. Add the paprika, stock, black pepper, and salt, toss, put the pan in the air fryer, and air fry at 190°C for 20 minutes. 4. Divide into bowls and serve.

Chapter 5 Seafood

Tasty Garlic Prawns

⏰ **Prep: 5 minutes**　🍴 **Cook: 12 minutes**　📚 **Serves: 4**

455g prawns
1 teaspoon cumin, ground
2 tablespoons parsley, chopped
2 tablespoons olive oil
A pinch of salt and black pepper
4 garlic cloves, minced
1 tablespoon lemon juice

1. Mix all the ingredients. 2. Place the prawns on the crisper plate in the basket. 3. Air-fry the food in the Ninja Air Fryer Max at 190°C for 12 minutes, tossing them halfway. 4. Divide into bowls and serve.
Per Serving: Calories 169; Fat 7.5g; Sodium 138mg; Carbs 2.73g; Fibre 0.4g; Sugar 0.7g; Protein 23.37g

Savoury Tuna Kabobs

⏰ **Prep: 5 minutes**　🍴 **Cook: 12 minutes**　📚 **Serves: 4**

455g tuna steaks, boneless and cubed
1 chili pepper, minced
4 green onions, chopped
2 tablespoons lime juice
A drizzle of olive oil
Salt and black pepper to the taste

1. Mix all ingredients in a bowl. 2. Thread the tuna cubes on skewers, arrange them on the crisper plate in the basket. 3. Air-fry the food in the Ninja Air Fryer Max at 190°C for 12 minutes. 4. Divide between plates and serve with a side salad.
Per Serving: Calories 128; Fat 1.47g; Sodium 292mg; Carbs 6.84g; Fibre 1.6g; Sugar 4.05g; Protein 23.22g

Crispy Fried Prawns

⏰ Prep: 15 minutes　🍳 Cook: 5 minutes　🍽 Serves: 4

65g self-rising flour
1 teaspoon paprika
1 teaspoon salt
½ teaspoon freshly ground black pepper
1 large egg, beaten
110g finely crushed panko bread crumbs
20 frozen large prawns, peeled and deveined
1 to 2 tablespoons oil
Pecan Tartar Sauce

1. In a shallow bowl, whisk the flour, paprika, salt, and pepper until blended. Add the beaten egg to a second shallow bowl and the bread crumbs to a third. 2. One at a time, dip the prawns into the flour, the egg, and the bread crumbs, coating thoroughly. 3. Line the crisper plate with parchment paper. Place the prawns on the crisper plate in the basket. 4. Air-fry the food in the Ninja Air Fryer Max at 200°C for 2 minutes. 5. Toss the prawns, spritz the prawns with oil, and cook for 3 minutes more until lightly browned and crispy. 6. Serve with pecan tartar sauce.

Per Serving: Calories 295; Fat 7.5g; Sodium 849mg; Carbs 46.98g; Fibre 10.7g; Sugar 19.99g; Protein 11.38g

Lemon Salmon Skewers

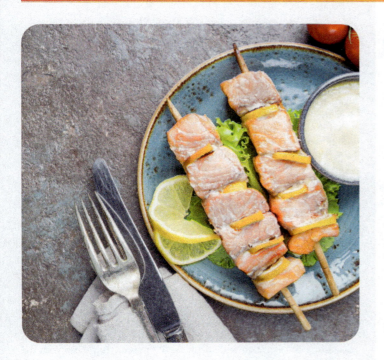

⏰ Prep: 10 minutes　🍳 Cook: 15 minutes　🍽 Serves: 4

455g wild salmon, skinless, boneless and cubed
2 lemons, sliced
60ml balsamic vinegar
60ml orange juice
100g orange marmalade
A pinch of salt and black pepper

1. Heat the vinegar in a pan over medium heat, add marmalade and orange juice, stir, bring to a simmer, cook for 1 minute and take off heat. 2. Thread salmon cubes and lemon slices on skewers, season with salt and black pepper, brush them with half of the orange marmalade mix. 3. Arrange the skewer onto the crisper plate in the basket. 4. Air-fry the food in the Ninja Air Fryer Max at 180°C for 3minutes. 5. Brush skewers with the rest of the vinegar mix, divide among plates and serve right away with a side salad. Enjoy!

Per Serving: Calories 501; Fat 1.32g; Sodium 28mg; Carbs 109.67g; Fibre 7.5g; Sugar 25.53g; Protein 17.28g

Salmon with Coconut Avocado Sauce

🕐 Prep: 10 minutes   🍲 Cook: 10 minutes   🍽 Serves: 4

1 avocado, pitted, peeled and chopped
4 salmon fillets, boneless
10g coriander, chopped
80ml coconut milk
1 tablespoon lime juice
1 tablespoon lime zest, grated
1 teaspoon onion powder
1 teaspoon garlic powder
Salt and black pepper to the taste

1. Season salmon fillets with salt, black pepper and lime zest, rub well, place them on the crisper plate in the basket. 2. Air-fry the food in the Ninja Air Fryer Max at 180°C for 9 minutes, flipping once and divide among plates. 3. In a food processor, mix avocado with coriander, garlic powder, onion powder, lime juice, salt, pepper and coconut milk, blend well, drizzle over salmon and serve right away.
Per Serving: Calories 612; Fat 27.06g; Sodium 207mg; Carbs 8.16g; Fibre 4.2g; Sugar 1.76g; Protein 81.68g

Garlic Prawns with Pasta Alfredo

🕐 Prep: 10 minutes   🍲 Cook: 55 minutes   🍽 Serves: 4

For the Garlic Prawns:
455g peeled small prawns, thawed if frozen
1 tablespoon olive oil
1 tablespoon minced garlic
¼ teaspoon sea salt
10g chopped fresh parsley
For the Pasta Alfredo:
200g no-boil lasagna noodles
480ml whole milk
60g heavy (whipping) cream
2 tablespoons unsalted butter, cut into small pieces
1 tablespoon minced garlic
½ teaspoon salt
¼ teaspoon freshly ground black pepper
50g grated Parmesan cheese

1. In a large bowl, combine the prawns, oil, garlic, and salt. 2. Break the lasagna noodles into 5cm pieces. Add the milk to the Zone 2 basket, then add the noodles, cream, butter, garlic, salt, and black pepper. Stir them well and ensure the pasta is fully submerged in the liquid. 3. Place the prawns on the crisper plate in the basket. Air-fry the food in the Ninja Air Fryer Max at 200°C for 13 minutes. 4. Place the pasta on the crisper plate in the basket. Bake the food in the Ninja Air Fryer Max at 180°C for 40 minutes 5. Transfer the pasta to a serving dish and stir in the Parmesan. Top them with the prawns and parsley.
Per Serving: Calories 416; Fat 18.54g; Sodium 1457mg; Carbs 36.08g; Fibre 0.3g; Sugar 15.96g; Protein 25.66g

Chapter 5 Seafood

Roasted Lemon Prawns

🕐 **Prep: 5 minutes**   🍲 **Cook: 12 minutes**   ♦ **Serves: 4**

675g prawns, peeled and deveined
Zest of ½ lemon, grated
Juice of ½ lemon
A pinch of salt and black pepper
2 tablespoons mustard
2 tablespoons olive oil
2 tablespoons parsley, chopped

1. In a bowl, mix all ingredients and toss well. 2. Put the prawns on the crisper plate in the basket and reserve the lemon vinaigrette. 3. Air-fry the food in the Ninja Air Fryer Max at 180°C for 12 minute, flipping the prawns halfway. 4. Divide the dish between plates and serve with reserved vinaigrette drizzled on top.
Per Serving: Calories 186; Fat 8.62g; Sodium 1075mg; Carbs 2.47g; Fibre 0.6g; Sugar 0.96g; Protein 23.77g

Crispy Fish with Potato Wedges

🕐 **Prep: 10 minutes**   🍲 **Cook: 45 minutes**   ♦ **Serves: 4**

For the Fish:
4 cod fillets (150g each)
4 tablespoons plain flour, divided
30g cornflour
1 teaspoon baking powder
¼ teaspoon salt
80ml lager-style beer or sparkling water
Tartar sauce, cocktail sauce, or malt vinegar, for serving (optional)

For the Potatoes:
4 russet potatoes
2 tablespoons vegetable oil
½ teaspoon paprika
½ teaspoon salt
¼ teaspoon garlic powder
¼ teaspoon freshly ground black pepper

1. Pat the fish dry with a paper towel and coat lightly with 2 tablespoons of flour. 2. In a shallow dish, combine the remaining 2 tablespoons of flour, the cornflour, baking powder, and salt. Stir in the beer to form a thick batter. 3. Dip the fish in the batter to coat both sides, then let rest on a cutting board for 10 minutes. 4. Cut each potato in half lengthwise, then cut each half into 4 wedges. 5. In a large bowl, combine the potatoes and oil. Toss well to fully coat the potatoes. Add the paprika, salt, garlic powder, and black pepper and toss well to coat. 6. Place a piece of parchment paper or aluminum foil over the plate. 7. Air-fry the fish in the Ninja Air Fryer Max at 200°C for 13 minutes, flipping the fish after 5 minutes of cooking time. 8. Place the potato wedges in a single layer on the crisper plate in the basket. Air-fry the food in the Ninja Air Fryer Max at 200°C for 30 minutes. 9. Serve hot with tartar sauce, cocktail sauce, or malt vinegar (if using).
Per Serving: Calories 660; Fat 22.53g; Sodium 873mg; Carbs 88.26g; Fibre 10.5g; Sugar 3.03g; Protein 28.41g

Chapter 5 Seafood | 49

Easy Roasted Sesame Prawns

⏰ **Prep: 5 minutes**   🍲 **Cook: 12 minutes**   📚 **Serves: 4**

455g prawns
A pinch of salt and black pepper
1 tablespoon sesame seeds, toasted
½ teaspoon Italian seasoning
Olive oil

1. In a bowl, mix the prawns with the rest of the ingredients and toss well. 2. Put the prawns on the crisper plate in the basket. 3. Air-fry the food in the Ninja Air Fryer Max at 190°C for 12 minutes. 4. Divide into bowls and serve.
Per Serving: Calories 115; Fat 1.83g; Sodium 162mg; Carbs 1.5g; Fibre 0.4g; Sugar 0.62g; Protein 23.44g

Rosemary Prawns with Cherry Tomatoes

⏰ **Prep: 5 minutes**   🍲 **Cook: 12 minutes**   📚 **Serves: 4**

455g prawns, peeled and deveined
150g cherry tomatoes
4 garlic cloves, minced
Salt and black pepper to the taste
1 tablespoon rosemary, chopped
2 tablespoons ghee, melted

1. Mix all the ingredients in a heatproof bowl or pan. 2. Put the pan on the crisper plate in the basket. Air-fry the food in the Ninja Air Fryer Max at 190°C for 12 minutes. 3. Divide into bowls and serve hot with asparagus if desired.
Per Serving: Calories 179; Fat 6.46g; Sodium 186mg; Carbs 7.6g; Fibre 1g; Sugar 5.24g; Protein 23.75g

Tender Garlic Cod Fish

⏲ **Prep: 15 minutes** 🍲 **Cook: 10 minutes** Servings: 2

2 cod fish fillets
1 tablespoon garlic, chopped
2 teaspoons swerve
2 tablespoons miso

1. Add all the recipe ingredients to the zip-lock bag. Shake well and store the bag in the refrigerator overnight. 2. Install the crisper plate in the air fryer basket and place the marinated fish fillets in the basket. Select Air Fry mode, and set the cooking temperature to 175°C, and adjust the cooking time to 10 minutes. Press the START/STOP to begin cooking. 3. Serve and enjoy.

Pesto Fish Finger Burgers

⏲ **Prep: 15 minutes** 🍲 **Cook: 15 minutes** Servings: 4

4 finger fish fillets
2 tablespoons flour
4 tomato slices
4 bread rolls
55g breadcrumbs
4 tablespoons pesto sauce
4 lettuce leaves
Black pepper and salt, to taste

1. Season the finger fish fillets with black pepper and salt, and coat them with the dry flour first; then dip in the breadcrumbs. 2. Place the crisper plate in the air fryer basket and grease with cooking spray. Arrange the fillets in the air fryer basket. Select Air Fry mode, set the cooking temperature to 185°C, and adjust the cooking time to 15 minutes. Press the START/STOP to begin cooking. 3. Cut the bread rolls in half. 4. Place a lettuce leaf on top of the bottom halves and top with a tomato slice; put the fillets over. 5. Spread a tablespoon of pesto sauce on top of each fillet, and top with the remaining halves. 6. Serve.

Lemony Breaded Fish Fillets

⏰ **Prep: 15 minutes**　🍲 **Cook: 12 minutes**　Servings: 4

30g breadcrumbs
4 tablespoon vegetable oil
1 egg
4 fish fillets
1 lemon

1. Mix the oil and breadcrumbs until crumbly. 2. Dip the prepared fish into the egg, then the crumb mixture. 3. Install the crisper plate in the air fryer basket and arrange the fish in the basket. Select Air Fry mode, then set the cooking temperature to 180°C, and adjust the cooking time to 12 minutes. Press the START/STOP to begin cooking. 4. Garnish using the lemon.

Garlic Butter Lobster Tails

⏰ **Prep: 15 minutes**　🍲 **Cook: 10 minutes**　Servings: 3

6 lobster tails
1 teaspoon garlic, minced
1 tablespoon butter
Black pepper and salt to taste
½ tablespoon lemon juice

1. Add all the recipe ingredients to a food processor, except the lobster, and blend well. 2. Clean the skin of the lobster and cover with the marinade. 3. Install the crisper plate in the air fryer basket and place the lobster in the basket. Select Air Fry mode, then set the cooking temperature 195°C, and adjust the cooking time to 10 minutes. Press the START/STOP to begin cooking. 4. Serve and enjoy!

Chapter 5 Seafood

Blackberry Glazed Salmon

⏰ Prep: 15 minutes 🍲 Cook: 12 minutes Servings: 2

2 salmon fillets, boneless
1 tablespoon honey
70g blackberries
1 tablespoon olive oil
Juice of ½ lemon
Black pepper and salt to taste

1. In a blender, mix the blackberries with the honey, oil, lemon juice, salt, and black pepper; pulse well. 2. Spread the blackberry mixture over the salmon. 3. Install the crisper plate in the air fryer basket and place the fish in the basket. Select Air Fry mode, set the cooking temperature to 195°C, and adjust the cooking time to 12 minutes. Press the START/STOP to begin cooking, flipping the fish halfway. 4. Serve hot and enjoy!

Spiced Catfish Fillets

⏰ Prep: 15 minutes 🍲 Cook: 13 minutes Servings: 4

4 catfish fillets
1 tablespoon olive oil
1 teaspoon paprika
1 teaspoon garlic powder
1 teaspoon dried basil
1 tablespoon Jamaican allspice, ground
½ lemon, juiced

1. In a suitable bowl, mix the paprika, garlic powder, and Jamaican allspice seasoning. 2. Rub the catfish fillets with the spice mixture. 3. Place the crisper plate in the air fryer basket and grease with cooking spray. Transfer the catfish fillets into the air fryer basket and drizzle with the olive oil. Select Air Fry mode, set the cooking temperature to 200°C, and adjust the cooking time to 7 minutes. Press the START/STOP to begin cooking. Turn the fillets and cook further for 6 minutes. 4. Serve sprinkled with the lemon juice.

Chapter 6 Meat

Beef and Sausage Meatballs

⏰ **Prep: 10 minutes** 🍲 **Cook: 20 minutes** ◆ **Serves: 4**

225g ground Italian sausage
225g 85% lean beef mince
50g shredded sharp cheddar cheese
½ teaspoon onion powder
½ teaspoon garlic powder
½ teaspoon black pepper

1. In a large bowl, gently mix the sausage, beef mince, cheese, onion powder, garlic powder, and pepper until well combined. 2. Form the mixture into 16 meatballs. 3. Place the meatballs in a single layer on the crisper plate in the basket. 4. Air-fry the food in the Ninja Air Fryer Max at 180°C for 20 minutes, turning the meatballs halfway through the cooking time. 5. Use a meat thermometer to ensure the meatballs have reached an internal temperature of 70°C (medium).
Per Serving: Calories 337; Fat 22.19g; Sodium 645mg; Carbs 6.57g; Fibre 1.8g; Sugar 0.08g; Protein 29.7g

Classic Meatloaf

⏰ **Prep: 10 minutes** 🍲 **Cook: 15 minutes** ◆ **Serves: 4**

455g 85% lean beef mince
2 large eggs, lightly beaten
160g diced yellow onion
10g chopped fresh coriander
1 tablespoon minced fresh ginger
1 tablespoon minced garlic
2 teaspoons Garam Masala
1 teaspoon salt
1 teaspoon ground turmeric
1 teaspoon cayenne pepper
½ teaspoon ground cinnamon
⅛ teaspoon ground cardamom

1. In a large bowl, gently mix the beef mince, eggs, onion, coriander, ginger, garlic, garam masala, salt, turmeric, cayenne, cinnamon, and cardamom until thoroughly combined. 2. Place the seasoned meat in a 20cm round baking pan with 10cm sides. 3. Place the pan on the crisper plate in the basket. 4. Air-fry the food in the Ninja Air Fryer Max at 180°C for 15 minutes. 5. Use a meat thermometer to ensure the meat loaf has reached an internal temperature of 70°C (medium). 6. Drain the fat and liquid from the pan and let stand for 5 minutes before slicing. 7. Slice and serve hot.
Per Serving: Calories 308; Fat 17.33g; Sodium 659mg; Carbs 4.09g; Fibre 1g; Sugar 1.14g; Protein 32.07

Kofta Kebabs

⏱ **Prep: 10 minutes**   🍲 **Cook: 10 minutes**   🍽 **Serves: 4**

455g 85% lean beef mince
10g chopped fresh parsley, plus more for garnish
2 tablespoons Kofta Kebab Spice Mix
1 tablespoon vegetable oil
1 tablespoon minced garlic
1 teaspoon salt

1. In the bowl of a stand mixer fitted with the paddle attachment, combine the beef mince, parsley, spice mix, vegetable oil, garlic, and salt. Mix on low speed until you have a sticky mess of spiced meat. If you have time, let the mixture stand at room temperature for 30 minutes (or cover and refrigerate for up to a day or two, until you're ready to make the kebabs). 2. Divide the meat into four equal portions. Form each into a long sausage shape. Place the kebabs in a single layer on the crisper plate in the basket. 3. Air-fry the food in the Ninja Air Fryer Max at 180°C for 10 minutes. 4. Use a meat thermometer to ensure the kebabs have reached an internal temperature of 70°C (medium). 5. Transfer the kebabs to a serving platter. Sprinkle with additional parsley and serve.

Per Serving: Calories 279; Fat 16.03g; Sodium 655mg; Carbs 1.52g; Fibre 0.2g; Sugar 0.22g; Protein 30.44g

Low-Carb Lasagna

⏱ **Prep: 10 minutes**   🍲 **Cook: 10 minutes**   🍽 **Serves: 4**

For the Meat Layer:
Extra-virgin olive oil
455g 85% lean beef mince
240ml prepared marinara sauce
30g diced celery
40g diced red onion
½ teaspoon minced garlic
Salt and black pepper

For the Cheese Layer:
200g ricotta cheese
120g shredded mozzarella cheese
50g grated Parmesan cheese
2 large eggs
1 teaspoon dried Italian seasoning, crushed
½ teaspoon each minced garlic, garlic powder, and black pepper

1. Grease a 20cm barrel cake tin with 1 teaspoon olive oil. 2. In a large bowl, combine the beef, marinara, celery, onion, garlic, salt, and pepper. Place the seasoned meat in the pan. 3. Place the pan on the crisper plate in the basket. 4. Air-fry the food in the Ninja Air Fryer Max at 190°C for 10 minutes. 5. In a medium bowl, combine the ricotta, the Parmesan, half the mozzarella, lightly beaten eggs, Italian seasoning, minced garlic, garlic powder, and pepper. Stir until well blended. 6. At the end of the cooking time, spread the cheese mixture over the meat mixture. Sprinkle with the remaining 60g mozzarella and continue to cook for 10 minutes until the cheese is browned and bubbling. 7. Use a meat thermometer to ensure the meat has reached an internal temperature of 70°C. 8. Drain the fat and liquid from the pan. Let stand for 5 minutes before serving.

Per Serving: Calories 576; Fat 35.83g; Sodium 1061mg; Carbs 11.11g; Fibre 1.7g; Sugar 3.99g; Protein 51.02g

Ham Mac 'N' Cheese

⏰ **Prep: 20 minutes**   🍳 **Cook: 25 minutes**   📚 **Serves: 4**

2 large eggs, beaten
480g cottage cheese, whole milk or 2%
200g grated sharp Cheddar cheese, divided
240g sour cream
½ teaspoon salt
1 teaspoon freshly ground black pepper
300g uncooked elbow macaroni
2 ham hocks (about 275g each), meat removed and diced
1 to 2 tablespoons oil

1. In a large bowl, stir together the eggs, cottage cheese, 100 g of the Cheddar cheese, sour cream, salt, and pepper. 2. Stir in the macaroni and the diced meat. 3. Spritz a suitable baking pan with oil. 4. Pour the macaroni mixture into the prepared pan, making sure all noodles are covered with sauce. 5. Air-fry the food in the Ninja Air Fryer Max at 180°C for 12 minutes. Stir in the remaining 100g of Cheddar cheese, making sure all the noodles are covered with sauce. 6. Cook for 13 minutes more, until the noodles are tender. 7. Let rest for 5 minutes before serving.
Per Serving: Calories 862; Fat 44.7g; Sodium 3147mg; Carbs 49.9g; Fibre 1.8g; Sugar 4.57g; Protein 64.16g

Air Fried Short Ribs

⏰ **Prep: 15 minutes**   🍳 **Cook: 20 minutes**   📚 **Serves: 4**

2 teaspoons smoked paprika
2 teaspoons packed brown sugar
1½ teaspoons ground cumin
Salt and pepper
675g short ribs, 3.5 to 5cm thick and 10 to 15cm long, trimmed
2 teaspoons plus 2 tablespoons extra-virgin olive oil
Relish:
35g finely chopped red pepper
1 small shallot, minced
2 garlic cloves, minced
Pinch cayenne pepper
2 tablespoons minced fresh coriander
2 teaspoons lemon juice

1. Combine the paprika, sugar, cumin, ½ teaspoon salt, and ¼ teaspoon pepper in bowl. 2. Pat the short ribs dry with paper towels, rub with 2 teaspoons oil, and sprinkle evenly with the spice mixture. 3. Arrange short ribs on the crisper plate in the basket. 4. Air-fry the food in the Ninja Air Fryer Max at 120°C for 18 to 24 minutes, flipping and rotating the short ribs halfway through cooking. 5. Transfer the short ribs to cutting board, tent with aluminum foil, and let rest while preparing the relish. 6. Microwave pepper, shallot, garlic, cayenne, ⅛ teaspoon salt, and remaining 2 tablespoons oil in bowl for 2 minutes until vegetables are softened, stirring occasionally. 7. Let the dish cool slightly, then stir in coriander and lemon juice. 8. Season the dish with salt and pepper to taste. Slice short ribs thin and serve with relish.
Per Serving: Calories 288; Fat 11.07g; Sodium 467mg; Carbs 31.63g; Fibre 3.5g; Sugar 15.43g; Protein 16.26g

Homemade Cheeseburgers

⏰ Prep: 10 minutes   🍲 Cook: 20 minutes   📚 Serves: 2

½ slice hearty white sandwich bread, crust removed, torn into ½cm pieces
1 tablespoon milk
½ teaspoon garlic powder
½ teaspoon onion powder
300g 85 percent lean beef mince
Salt and pepper
2 slices American cheese
2 hamburger buns, toasted if desired

1. Mash bread, milk, garlic powder, and onion powder into paste in medium bowl using fork. 2. Break up beef mince into small pieces over bread mixture in bowl and lightly knead with hands until well combined. 3. Divide mixture into 2 lightly packed balls, then gently flatten each into 2.5cm-thick patty. 4. Press centre of each patty with fingertips to create ½ cm-deep depression. Season with salt and pepper. 5. Arrange patties on the crisper plate in the basket. 6. Air-fry the food in the Ninja Air Fryer Max at 180°C for 21 minutes, flipping and rotating burgers halfway through cooking. 7. Top each burger with 1 slice cheese. Return basket to Ninja Air Fryer Max and cook until cheese is melted, about 30 seconds. 8. Serve burgers on buns.

Per Serving: Calories 583; Fat 35.95g; Sodium 1360mg; Carbs 11.06g; Fibre 1.4g; Sugar 5.18g; Protein 51.21g

Authentic Carne Asada

⏰ Prep: 10 minutes   🍲 Cook: 10 minutes   📚 Serves: 4

Juice of 2 limes
1 orange, peeled and seeded
40g fresh coriander leaves
1 jalapeño, diced
2 tablespoons vegetable oil
2 tablespoons apple cider vinegar
2 teaspoons ancho chile powder
2 teaspoons sugar
1 teaspoon salt
1 teaspoon cumin seeds
1 teaspoon coriander seeds
675g skirt steak, cut into 3 pieces

1. In a blender, combine the lime juice, coriander, orange, jalapeño, vegetable oil, vinegar, chile powder, sugar, salt, cumin, and coriander. Blend until smooth. 2. Put the steak in a resealable plastic bag. Add the marinade over the steak and seal the bag. Let stand at room temperature for 30 minutes or cover and refrigerate for up to 24 hours. 3. Place the steak pieces on the crisper plate in the basket. 4. Air-fry the food in the Ninja Air Fryer Max at 200°C for 8 minutes. 5. Use a meat thermometer to ensure the steak has reached an internal temperature of 75°C. 6. Transfer the steak to a cutting board and let rest for 10 minutes. Slice across the grain and serve.

Per Serving: Calories 473; Fat 27.63g; Sodium 714mg; Carbs 9.51g; Fibre 1.5g; Sugar 5.37g; Protein 45.36g

Simple Pork Bulgogi

⏰ Prep: 10 minutes   🍲 Cook: 15 minutes   ❖ Serves: 4

1 onion, thinly sliced
2 tablespoons gochujang (Korean red chili paste)
1 tablespoon minced fresh ginger
1 tablespoon minced garlic
1 tablespoon soy sauce
1 tablespoon rice cooking wine
1 tablespoon toasted sesame oil
1 teaspoon sugar
¼ to 1 teaspoon cayenne pepper or gochugaru (Korean ground red pepper)
455g boneless pork shoulder, cut into 1 cm-thick slices
1 tablespoon sesame seeds
25g sliced spring onions

1. In a large bowl, combine the onion, gochujang, ginger, garlic, soy sauce, wine, sesame oil, sugar, and cayenne. Add the pork and toss to coat. Marinate at room temperature for 30 minutes, or cover and refrigerate for up to 24 hours. 2. Arrange the pork and onion slices on the crisper plate in the basket. 3. Air-fry the food in the Ninja Air Fryer Max at 200°C for 15 minutes, turning the pork halfway through the cooking time. 4. Place the pork on a serving platter. Sprinkle with the sesame seeds and spring onions and serve.
Per Serving: Calories 209; Fat 11.49g; Sodium 1342mg; Carbs 7.01g; Fibre 0.9g; Sugar 4.93g; Protein 20.43g

Crispy Parmesan Pork Chops

⏰ Prep: 15 minutes   🍲 Cook: 12 minutes   Servings: 6

680g pork chops, boneless
1 teaspoon paprika
1 teaspoon creole seasoning
1 teaspoon garlic powder
25g parmesan cheese, grated
40g almond flour

1. Add all the recipe ingredients except pork chops in a zip-lock bag. 2. Add pork chops in the bag. Seal this bag and shake well to coat pork chops. 3. Install the crisper plate in the air fryer basket. Remove pork chops from the zip-lock bag and place in the air fryer basket. 4. Cook pork chops at 180°C for 10-12 minutes. 5. Serve and enjoy.

Lamb Patties with Feta

⏱ **Prep: 15 minutes**   🍲 **Cook: 20 minutes**   Servings: 4

680g ground lamb
35g feta cheese, crumbled
1 teaspoon oregano
¼ teaspoon black pepper
½ teaspoon salt

1. Add all the recipe ingredients into the bowl and mix until well combined. 2. Make the equal shape of patties from the meat mixture. 3. Install the crisper plate in the air fryer basket and place the lamb patties in the basket. 4. Select Air Fry mode, set the cooking temperature to 190°C, and adjust the cooking time to 20 minutes. Press the START/STOP to begin cooking. Flip halfway through the cooking time. 5. Serve and enjoy.

Walnut-Crusted Pork Tenderloin

⏱ **Prep: 15 minutes**   🍲 **Cook: 15 minutes**   Servings: 4

3 tablespoons grainy mustard
2 teaspoons olive oil
¼ teaspoon dry mustard powder
455g pork tenderloin, excess fat trimmed
2 slices whole-wheat bread, crumbled
20g ground walnuts
2 tablespoons cornstarch

1. In a suitable bowl, stir together the mustard, olive oil, and mustard powder. Spread this mixture over the pork. 2. On a plate, mix the bread crumbs, walnuts, and cornstarch. Dip the mustard-coated pork into the crumb mixture to coat. 3. Install the crisper plate in the air fryer basket and place the pork in the basket. Select Air Fry mode, set the cooking temperature to 195°C, and adjust the cooking time to 15 minutes. Press the START/STOP to begin cooking. Flip halfway through the cooking time. Cook until it registers at least 60°C on a meat thermometer. 4. Slice to serve.

Perfect Beef Roast

⏰ **Prep: 15 minutes**　🍲 **Cook: 35 minutes**　Servings: 7

905g beef roast
1 tablespoon olive oil
1 teaspoon thyme
2 teaspoons garlic powder
¼ teaspoon black pepper
1 tablespoon kosher salt

1. Coat roast with olive oil. 2. Mix together thyme, black pepper, garlic powder, and salt and rub all over the roast. 3. Install the crisper plate in the air fryer basket and place the roast in the basket. Select Air Roast mode, set the cooking temperature to 200°C, and adjust the cooking time to 20 minutes. Press the START/STOP to begin cooking. 4. Coat the roast with cooking spray and cook for 15 minutes more. 5. Slice and serve.

Juicy Garlic Butter Steak

⏰ **Prep: 15 minutes**　🍲 **Cook: 6 minutes**　Servings: 2

2 steaks
2 teaspoon garlic butter
¼ teaspoon Italian seasoning
Black pepper
Salt

1. Season steaks with Italian seasoning, black pepper, and salt. 2. Place the crisper plate in the air fryer basket. Rub steaks with garlic butter and place the steaks in the basket. Select Air Roast mode, set the cooking temperature to 175°C, and adjust the cooking time to 6 minutes. Press the START/STOP to begin cooking. 3. Serve and enjoy.

Air Fryer Marinated Steak

⏰ **Prep: 15 minutes**   🍲 **Cook: 7 minutes**   Servings: 2

340g steaks
½ tablespoon unsweetened cocoa powder
1 tablespoon Montreal steak seasoning
1 teaspoon liquid smoke
1 tablespoon soy sauce
Black pepper
Salt

1. Add steak, liquid smoke, and soy sauce in a zip-lock bag and shake well. 2. Season the steak with seasonings and refrigerate it overnight. 3. Install the crisper plate in the air fryer basket and place the marinated steak in the basket. Select Air Roast mode, set the cooking temperature to 190°C, and adjust the cooking time to 5 minutes. Press the START/STOP to begin cooking. Turn the steak to another side and cook for 2 minutes more. 4. Serve and enjoy.

Chapter 6 Meat | 61

Chapter 7 Desserts

Yummy Black 'n' White Brownies

⏱ **Prep: 10 minutes** 🍲 **Cook: 20 minutes** ⬢ **Serves: 12**

1 egg
55g brown sugar
2 tablespoons white sugar
65g plain flour
40g white chocolate chips
2 tablespoons safflower oil
1 teaspoon vanilla
20g cocoa powder
Cooking spray

1. In a large bowl, beat the egg, brown sugar, and white sugar until smooth. Add the vanilla and safflower oil; mix well. 2. Slowly pour in the flour and cocoa powder, and whisk until combined. Add the white chocolate chips, stirring gently to combine. 3. Grease a suitable baking pan with cooking spray. Spread the mixture into the baking pan and place the pan on the crisper plate in the basket. 4. Bake the food in the Ninja Air Fryer Max at 180°C for 20 minutes until a knife inserted in the centre comes out clean. 5. Transfer to a large dish and let cool completely before serving.
Per Serving: Calories 90; Fat 4.48g; Sodium 13mg; Carbs 11.72g; Fibre 0.6g; Sugar 7.98g; Protein 1.64g

Orange Polenta Cake

⏱ **Prep: 10 minutes** 🍲 **Cook: 20 minutes** ⬢ **Serves: 8**

300ml orange juice
50g polenta
150g white sugar
165g plain flour
60ml safflower oil
30g icing sugar
1 teaspoon vanilla
1 teaspoon baking soda
Cooking spray

1. Grease a suitable baking pan with cooking spray. Set aside. 2. In a small bowl, mix together the safflower oil, polenta, flour, sugar, baking soda, vanilla, and 240ml orange juice. 3. Spoon the mixture into the prepared pan and place the pan into the Ninja Air Fryer Max basket. 4. Put the food on the crisper plate in the basket. 5. Bake the food in the Ninja Air Fryer Max at 190°C for 24 minutes until the cake is golden brown. 6. Transfer to wire racks to cool. Make about 20 holes in the baked cake with a toothpick. Set aside. 7. In a small bowl, whisk the icing sugar and remaining orange juice. Pour over the cake slowly for a good soak. 8. Simply cut the cake into wedges before serving.
Per Serving: Calories 230; Fat 10.78g; Sodium 160mg; Carbs 30.09g; Fibre 1.4g; Sugar 8.38g; Protein 3.28g

Sweet Banana Cake

⏰ **Prep: 15 minutes** 🍲 **Cook: 30 minutes** 🍽 **Serves: 4**

2 tablespoons honey
1 banana, mashed
75g brown sugar
3½ tablespoons butter, at room temperature
1 egg, beaten
½ teaspoon ground cinnamon
125g self-raising flour
A pinch of salt
Cooking spray

1. In a bowl, mix the sugar and butter together with an electric mixer until smooth. Set aside. 2. In another bowl, combine the banana, beaten egg, and honey. Stir the banana mixture into the sugar mixture until smooth. 3. Spritz a pan with the cooking spray. Add the cinnamon, flour, and salt to banana-butter mixture. Stir well. Spread the mixture evenly on the pan with a spatula. 4. Place the pan on the crisper plate in the basket. 5. Bake the food in the Ninja Air Fryer Max at 160°C for 30 minutes or until a toothpick inserted into the cake comes out clean. 6. Remove the pan from the basket. Transfer the cake to a platter. Let stand for 5 minutes before serving.

Per Serving: Calories 360; Fat 12.89g; Sodium 523mg; Carbs 56.91g; Fibre 1.8g; Sugar 30.09g; Protein 5.83g

Chocolate Chip Cookies

⏰ **Prep: 10 minutes** 🍲 **Cook: 10 minutes** 🍽 **Serves: 6**

1 tablespoon refined coconut oil, melted
1 tablespoon maple syrup
1 tablespoon nondairy milk
½ teaspoon vanilla
30g plus 2 tablespoons whole-wheat pastry flour or plain gluten-free flour
2 tablespoons coconut sugar
¼ teaspoon sea salt
¼ teaspoon baking powder
2 tablespoons vegan chocolate chips
Cooking oil spray (sunflower, safflower, or refined coconut)

1. In a medium bowl, stir together the oil, maple syrup, milk, and vanilla. Add the flour, coconut sugar, salt, and baking powder. Stir just until thoroughly combined. Stir in the chocolate chips. 2. Spray the pan lightly with oil. 3. Drop tablespoonfuls of the batter onto the pan, leaving a little room in between in case they spread out a bit. 4. Bake the food in the Ninja Air Fryer Max at 180°C for 7 minutes, or until lightly browned. Be careful not to overcook. 5. Gently transfer to a cooling rack (or plate). Repeat as desired, making all of the cookies at once, or keeping the batter on hand in the fridge to be used later. 6. Enjoy warm if possible!

Per Serving: Calories 107; Fat 4.59g; Sodium 138mg; Carbs 15.57g; Fibre 0.4g; Sugar 7.74g; Protein 1.11g

Chocolate Chip Macadamia Nut Cookies

⏰ **Prep: 15 minutes**　🍲 **Cook: 15 minutes**　Servings: 4

1 egg
3 tablespoons butter
1 teaspoon vanilla
¼ teaspoon baking powder
2 tablespoons macadamia nuts, crushed
110g almond flour
2 tablespoon unsweetened chocolate chips
Pinch of salt

1. In a suitable bowl, beat the egg with a hand mixer. 2. Stir in the almond flour, vanilla, butter, baking powder, and salt and stir well. 3. Add the chocolate chips and macadamia nuts and mix until dough is formed. Make the cookies from dough. 4. Install the crisper plate in the air fryer basket and arrange the cookies in basket. Select Bake mode, and set the cooking temperature at 180°C and adjust the cooking time to 15 minutes. Press the START/STOP to begin cooking. 5. Serve and enjoy.

Coconut Cream Cheese Muffins

⏰ **Prep: 15 minutes**　🍲 **Cook: 10 minutes**　Servings: 8

1 egg
1 teaspoon baking soda
110g almond flour
2 tablespoons coconut flakes
2 teaspoons erythritol
1 teaspoon vinegar
230g cream cheese
Pinch of salt

1. Beat the cream cheese and egg in a suitable bowl until well combined. 2. Add the almond flour, vinegar, coconut flakes, baking soda, sweetener, and salt and beat until well combined. 3. Pour the batter into the silicone muffin moulds and place into the air fryer. 4. Bake at 180°C for almost 10 minutes. 5. Serve and enjoy.

Chocolate Soufflé

⏲ **Prep: 15 minutes** 🍲 **Cook: 12 minutes** Servings: 6

3 eggs, separated
1 teaspoon vanilla
50g swerve
5 tablespoons butter, melted
2 tablespoons of heavy cream
2 tablespoons almond flour
55g dark chocolate, melted

1. Mix together melted chocolate and butter. 2. In a suitable bowl, whisk egg yolk with sweetener until combined. 3. Add almond flour, heavy cream, and vanilla and whisk well. 4. In a separate bowl, whisk egg whites until soft peaks form. 5. Slowly add the egg white to the chocolate mixture and fold well. 6. Pour the chocolate mixture into the ramekins and place them into the air fryer. 7. Bake at 165°C for 12 minutes. 8. Serve and enjoy.

Mini Chocolate Cake

⏲ **Prep: 15 minutes** 🍲 **Cook: 13 minutes** Servings: 4

1½ tablespoons almond flour
100g unsalted butter
100g sugar-free dark chocolate, chopped
2 eggs
3½ tablespoons swerve

1. Microwave all chocolate bits with butter in a suitable bowl for about 3 minutes. 2. Remove this melt from the microwave, whisk in the eggs and swerve. 3. Add the flour and mix well until smooth. 4. Grease four regular-sized ramekins. Transfer the mixture into the ramekins and arrange in the air fryer basket. 5. Bake at 190°C for 10 minutes and dish out to serve.

Vanilla Butter Cake

⏰ **Prep: 15 minutes**   🍲 **Cook: 35 minutes**   Servings: 8

6 egg yolks
335g almond flour
2 teaspoons vanilla
1 egg, lightly beaten
50g erythritol
225g butter
Pinch of salt

1. In a suitable bowl, beat butter and sweetener until fluffy. 2. Add vanilla and egg yolks and beat until well combined. 3. Add remaining ingredients and beat until combined. 4. Pour batter into an air fryer cake pan and place into the air fryer and cook at 175°C for 35 minutes. 5. Slice and serve.

Easy Peanut Butter Cookies

⏰ **Prep: 15 minutes**   🍲 **Cook: 12 minutes**   Servings: 5

1 egg
50g erythritol
255g peanut butter

1. Add all ingredients into a bowl and mix until well combined. 2. Make the cookies from the mixture and place them into the air fryer. Bake at 160°C and cook for 12 minutes. 3. Serve and enjoy.

Chapter 7 Desserts

Conclusion

As you reach the end of the Ninja Air Fryer Max XL Cookbook, we hope you feel inspired and equipped to explore the endless possibilities this remarkable appliance offers. With its ability to create healthier versions of your favourite dishes, the Ninja Air Fryer Max XL is not just a cooking tool; it's a gateway to a more enjoyable and balanced way of eating.

Throughout this cookbook, we've shared a variety of recipes that cater to different tastes and dietary needs, all designed to help you make the most of your air fryer. Whether you're whipping up a quick midweek meal or impressing guests at a dinner party, you now have the knowledge and skills to create delicious, crispy dishes that are sure to delight.

We encourage you to continue experimenting and personalising your recipes, embracing the creativity that comes with cooking. Remember, each meal is an opportunity to enjoy fresh flavours and share memorable moments with loved ones. Thank you for choosing this cookbook as your guide; may your culinary adventures with the Ninja Air Fryer Max XL bring you joy and satisfaction for years to come!

Appendix Recipes Index

A

Air Fried Scotch Eggs 21
Air Fried Short Ribs 56
Air Fried Vegetable Skewers 23
Air Fryer Crispy Whole Chicken Wings 43
Air Fryer Marinated Steak 61
Almond-Crusted Chicken Nuggets 41
Apple Pancakes 19
Authentic Carne Asada 57

B

Bacon and Eggs Breakfast 15
Bacon-Wrapped Sausage 30
Baked Pecan French Toast 17
Balsamic Roasted Brussels Sprouts 35
Beef and Sausage Meatballs 54
Blackberry Glazed Salmon 53
Broccoli Cheddar Casserole 31
Buffalo Cauliflower Florets 33
Buttermilk Fried Chicken Breasts 42
Buttermilk Fried Chicken Wings 43

C

Cajun Chicken Breasts 38
Cauliflower Pizza Crust 25
Cheese and Sausage Quiche 16
Cheese Drop Biscuits 35
Cheese Soufflés with Mushrooms 25
Cheese Tomato Frittata 18
Cheesy Bacon Egg Muffins 15
Cheesy Cauliflower Bites 34
Cheesy Chicken and Courgette Casserole 39
Cheesy Egg Stuffed Peppers 21
Chocolate Chip Cookies 63
Chocolate Chip Macadamia Nut Cookies 64
Chocolate Soufflé 65
Classic Meatloaf 54
Coconut Cream Cheese Muffins 64
Courgette Fritters 26
Crispy Chicken Nuggets 42
Crispy Fish with Potato Wedges 49
Crispy Flax Cheddar Cheese Chips 31
Crispy Fried Prawns 47
Crispy Mozzarella Cheese Sticks 32

Crispy Parmesan Pork Chops 58
Crispy Popcorn Chicken 44
Crispy Turnip Fries 24
Crunchy Spanish Peanuts 36

D

Delicious Chicken Breasts 41

E

Easy Marinated Chicken Wings 40
Easy Peanut Butter Cookies 66
Easy Roasted Sesame Prawns 50

F

Flavourful Buffalo Chicken Wings 40
Flavourful Cheese Onion Risotto 17
Fluffy Cloud Eggs 30
Fluffy Corn Bread 20

G

Garlic Broccoli with Sriracha 28
Garlic Butter Lobster Tails 52
Garlic Prawns with Pasta Alfredo 48
Garlic Roasted Cherry Tomatoes 29
Garlicky Radish Chips 32
Glazed Ham Steak 22

H

Ham Mac 'N' Cheese 56
Healthy Tamari Green Beans 28
Homemade Cheeseburgers 57
Homemade Pork Patties 20
Homemade Roasted Brussels Sprouts with Bacon 26

J

Juicy Garlic Butter Steak 60

K

Kofta Kebabs 55

L

Lamb Patties with Feta 59
Lemon Roasted Whole Chicken 44
Lemon Salmon Skewers 47
Lemony Breaded Fish Fillets 52
Low-Carb Lasagna 55

M

Marinated Chicken Drumsticks 38
Mini Chocolate Cake 65

N

Nut and Berry Granola 22

O

Orange Polenta Cake 62

P

Perfect Beef Roast 60
Pesto Fish Finger Burgers 51
Pigs in a Blanket 36
Prosciutto-Wrapped Asparagus 27

R

Roasted Brussels Sprouts 29
Roasted Lemon Prawns 49
Roasted Taco Cauliflower 33
Rosemary Potato Chips with Sour Cream 34
Rosemary Prawns with Cherry Tomatoes 50

S

Salmon with Coconut Avocado Sauce 48
Savoury Tuna Kabobs 46
Scrambled Eggs with Mushrooms 19
Shakshuka Harissa 37
Simple Courgette Ribbons 27
Simple Pork Bulgogi 58
Spiced Catfish Fillets 53
Spicy Chicken Wings 39
Spinach and Cheese Quiche 16
Sweet Banana Cake 63
Sweet Cranberry Muffins 18

T

Tasty Cheese Spinach Frittata 23
Tasty Garlic Prawns 46
Tasty Masala Omelet 37
Tender Garlic Cod Fish 51
Tomato Avocado Boats 24
Turkey Breasts with Shallot 45

V

Vanilla Butter Cake 66

W

Walnut-Crusted Pork Tenderloin 59

Y

Yummy Black 'n' White Brownies 62

Printed in Great Britain
by Amazon